Murder by Gaslight

IN VICTORIAN BRADFORD

MARK DAVIS

AMBERLEY PUBLISHING

Acknowledgements

I would like to express my gratitude to the following:

Sue Caton and her colleagues at the Bradford Local Studies Library.
Bradford Archive Services.
Joseph Pettican and Elizabeth Watts at Amberley Publishing for their help and assistance in compiling this book, our seventh collaboration.
Particular thanks, as always, to my partner Marina Kidd for all her support and assistance in the making of this book.

First published 2013

Amberley Publishing
The Hill, Stroud, Gloucestershire, GL5 4EP
www.amberley-books.com

Copyright © Mark Davis, 2013

The right of Mark Davis to be identified as the
Author of this work has been asserted in accordance with
the Copyrights, Designs and Patents Act 1988.

ISBN 978 1 4456 2281 1 (print)
ISBN 978 1 4456 2295 8 (ebook)

British Library Cataloguing in Publication Data.
A catalogue record for this book is available from the
British Library.

Typesetting by Amberley Publishing.
Printed and bound in the UK by CPI Colour.

Contents

Acknowledgements   2

Introduction   4

Samuel Charlton, Murder and Suicide, 1857   6

Margaret Sutton (Gowland), Double Murder and Suicide, 1860   13

Francis William Neale, Wife Murder, 1888   29

James Kirkby, Double Murder and Suicide, 1888   47

James Harrison, Wife Murder, 1890   57

Thomas Bentley, Murder and Suicide, 1894   69

Lister Bastow, Double Murder and Suicide, 1897   77

The Bradford Midland Hotel, Murder or Suicide, 1897   87

Introduction

If you are looking for a nice bedtime book to read, then I suggest you put this one down. Unlike my previous publication, *Bradford Through Time*, which explored Bradford's rich historical landscape, this book focuses on some of the lives that were deeply affected by living conditions at a time when Bradford virtually controlled the woollen industry. During the Industrial Revolution, Bradford was to become the textile capital of the world, earning the town the nickname 'Worstedopolis'. Many of the mills around Bradford produced a fine woollen fabric more commonly known as 'worsted', which brought in vast fortunes for the wool barons who owned and controlled the mills. You only have to visit the magnificent promenade at Undercliffe Cemetery where, set in stone, their former wealth and influence is expressed by huge ornate monuments that still dominate the skyline today. However, the success of these men was set against a backdrop of misery, suffering and exploitation. Millworkers worked long hours in dangerous conditions for small wages; their graves reflect their inferior status, and are mostly unmarked and positioned on the boundaries of the cemetery.

Within this book, I have detailed previously unpublished accounts of human suffering, and each and every one of them ends in death. When I first started to put this book together, my intention was not to produce 'yet another murder book' where the facts have been edited down to a bare minimum, and I feel that I have remained true to that ideal. This book not only explores the circumstances surrounding every tragedy, it also gives the reader a true representation of the facts as well as an insight into life in Victorian Bradford. The stories recounted are horrific to say the least, and there is no romance between these pages. I have no doubt many will find the stories harrowing and upsetting, but I suspect that a few may seek out certain graves, such as that of Margaret Sutton, who, in a fit of despair, took the lives of her two young daughters before killing herself. Margaret's story is an extreme example of how Victorian morality affected the population.

As you make your way through the book, try to imagine a Britain with no welfare state, where the creature comforts we take for granted were a thing of the future, where children aged just ten were sent to the mill as half-timers, where whole families shared one double bed and where life on the poverty line was brutal and demoralising. A friend of mine once told me 'you can help someone with depression but there is no helping someone in despair'. This book is full of despair; in some cases, normally placid people are driven by circumstances they cannot control to take the lives of their wives, children and even themselves. The majority of murders in Bradford were of a domestic nature, and this was also indicative of other towns during the same period.

The contemporary newspapers of the day, such as the *Bradford Daily Telegraph* and the *Bradford Observer*, were incredibly detailed when relating to crime, and especially murder in the nineteenth century; every slash, cut and hammer blow was recorded minutely for the general public, who were forever eager to consume every morsel of information. It is from those nineteenth-century newspaper articles that much of the information contained within this book has been drawn. Not only do we visit long gone crime scenes, but we also become spectators at inquests, trials and even funerals. In addition, I have managed to source many contemporary illustrations, which, along with more recent images, assist us in seeing the bigger picture.

Every story recounted in this book left families reeling for decades after the event. Take, for example, Lister Bastow, who killed his wife and daughter because he simply could not cope with his wife leaving him when poverty brought the family to imminent eviction. His actions left his two younger children orphaned, as was the case with Hannah Holroyd's family when Samuel Charlton, full of jealousy, virtually decapitated her rather than see her leave him for a much younger man.

The long dead victims of these horrific crimes have, through the medium of this book, been given recognition and a voice. They are no longer silenced by the sheer passage of time.

Mark Davis

Samuel Charlton
Murder and Suicide, 1857

DREADFUL MURDER AND SUICIDE AT LIDGET GREEN

The quiet and rural locality of Lidget Green was at midnight on Monday the scene of a dreadful murder, which was quickly followed by the deliberate suicide of the murderer. The murderer was Samuel Charlton, 68 years of age, and his victim was Hannah Holroyd, aged 42. They were persons in a humble condition. Charlton was an assistant to bailiffs, and a person of very indifferent character. He was a widower, and had five or six children, all of them being able to maintain themselves. Hannah Holroyd was a widow, and had five children, the youngest of which was under five years of age.

They both resided in the same street – Club Street – at Lidget Green; the cottage of one being nearly opposite that of the other.

Since Whitsuntide last, an intimacy partaking of the character of courtship has sustained between Charlton and Mrs Holroyd, the former going regularly to the house of the latter, and being frequently seen with her abroad in the neighbourhood, as well as in Bradford. Some differences had, however, latterly arisen between them, on account of Mrs Holroyd favouring the advances of a rival suitor who appeared a much younger man, Luke Normington, aged 30, who had just returned from serving in the militia.

Bradford Observer
14 May 1857

The Murder

When the object of Samuel Charlton's affections directed her gaze to a much younger man than himself, he was absolutely livid. To say he was jealous was an understatement. At twenty-six years his junior, Hannah Holroyd was a good catch for the wiry old pensioner, and he was not prepared to let her waltz off in the arms of a man thirty-eight years younger than himself without a damn good fight. Even if it meant Hannah's five children – the youngest just four years old – would be orphaned, he would have his satisfaction. It was a clear case of 'if I cannot have you, then nobody can'. Once the deed was done, Charlton, possibly feeling the enormity of his self-inflicted loss, put an end to his own life. Or it might just be that he took the coward's way out, thus denying the hangman his rightful fee. Either way, Charlton was not prepared to take responsibility for his atrocious actions.

Club Street, Lidget Green.

On Monday 11 May 1857, Charlton and the widowed Mrs Holroyd attended the local evening Temperance meeting. At first, it was thought they had gone together; later testimony dispelled this rumour for, in fact, during the meeting the once intimate couple were seated at a distance from each other. It was further claimed that Charlton was abstaining from drink and had done for some time, but he had in fact fallen off the wagon only a month after signing the pledge. At the conclusion of the meeting, Charlton and Mrs Holroyd walked together back to Club Street, just off Cemetery Road. Along the way, they encountered his younger rival, Luke Normington. It is not known what conversation took place at this time between them, but we do know that Charlton walked off, making his way to Mrs Holroyd's house. Mrs Holroyd, after leaving Luke, went to visit a neighbour before returning home at around 11.30 p.m., but not before meeting with Luke once more. It would seem that Charlton was not in the mood for talking as he sat by the fire awaiting Hannah's return, and appeared to be in a sullen mood, which was witnessed by Hannah's eldest daughter, Martha, who was nineteen years old. Martha left the couple, who were sitting in complete silence, to go to bed at around 11.45 p.m. What happened before the murder was discovered, we will never know. There was no witness that could recall a single scream or raised word as Hannah was butchered to death.

At 12.30 a.m., Martha was awakened by the sound of the front door opening. She then heard the door closing quietly, and the departing footsteps of Charlton. Seeing a light coming from downstairs, Martha supposed that her mother, who slept on the ground floor, had fallen asleep, leaving the candle burning. Martha immediately went downstairs with the intention of locking the door and putting out the light. Having bolted the door, she turned around and was aghast to discover the body of her mother lying in a pool of blood on the opposite side of the room. The frantic screams of 'murder' pierced the evening silence, and were heard by a policeman and several neighbours, who wasted no time in coming to her assistance.

The first on the scene was PC Reuben Binns, who was in the immediate vicinity. Arriving in Club Street, he identified the source of the disturbance, only to find the door locked from the inside. As Martha unlocked the door, PC Binns quickly entered the cottage, closely followed by neighbours Abraham Pearson and Henry Jowett. What they saw left them horrified, for so vicious was the attack on Hannah that her head was nearly completely severed. On closer inspection of the body, PC Binns also detected a small cut to the victim's right hand, which he attributed to Hannah attempting to defend herself. After ascertaining that the prime suspect was Samuel Charlton, who had recently left the crime scene, the constable crossed the road to Charlton's house to arrest him. Unfortunately, the object of the constable's suspicions had left his house in a hurry just a quarter of an hour previously. Ellen Dyson, Charlton's daughter, greeted PC Binns at the door and informed him that her father had come to her bedside in a distressed state. He had shaken hands with his children saying, 'Farewell, you will never see me again,' before departing. On leaving, she heard him return for a moment and lift up the cellar grate, and then go on his way. On inspecting the cellar, Binns found a razor, covered in blood.

With the evidence of the cowardly murder solidly pointing to Samuel Charlton, PC Binns, Sergeant John Knowles and Constable Jowett searched the local neighbourhood. By this time, a large number of people had gathered around the murder scene as news of the tragedy spread far and wide. They soon came to the conclusion that Charlton might kill himself by drowning. With this in mind, the search was extended beyond the fields in the immediate vicinity to the mill dams and the streams. At around 4 a.m. on the Tuesday morning as the search party made its way down Thief Score Lane, a hat was spotted floating in the upper part of New Miller's Dam. The members of the party then concentrated their efforts around the dam and further investigation confirmed their worst fears. Charlton's body was discovered by Sergeant Knowles, floating in an upright position, his feet not quite touching the bottom, some four or five yards from the edge. Once recovered, his remains were taken to the New Miller's Dam public house on Thornton Road.

The Investigation

The inquest for Hannah Holroyd was held at the Second West public house, on the corner of Cemetery Road, Lidget Green, just a short distance from the murder scene on Wednesday 13 May. The coroner Mr George Dyson swore in the following jury: Mr Edwin Bentley, foreman, Mr Francis Ackroyd, Mr Alexander Wild, Mr Joshua Horsfall, Mr John Hudson, Mr Jonas Jennings, Mr Aaron Topham, Mr Benjamin Crabtree, Mr William Wardle, Mr Charles Fox, Mr Henry Suddards, Mr Walton, and Mr Jeremiah Rudd.

Martha Holroyd, the daughter of the deceased, was the first witness called. She said, 'I am 19 years of age. I work at Mr John Turner's mill. I am daughter of Hannah Holroyd, the deceased. My father, Joshua Holroyd, died about five years ago. He was a quarryman. There are five children – the youngest is about four years of age. I knew Samuel Charlton. He had no trade; he was a sort of bailiff. I don't know if he intended to marry my mother; but he has been in the habit of coming in and sitting in our house. He has not been well received for some time past; she did not take him in properly. He had never threatened to do her injury in my hearing. I saw him on Monday evening about seven o'clock. My mother went to a teetotal meeting at Lidget Green. She came home from the meeting about half past eleven.' Martha then went on to describe the circumstances surrounding her mother's murder before adding, 'My mother rather leaned to Luke. He met her as she was coming from a neighbouring house, on Monday night, and "clicked" hold of her. I went for her and saw him stop her. Charlton was at that time at her house. My mother was nearly undressed at the time she was found. I don't know that Charlton ever stopped all night. Luke Normington had been two or three times at our house, but he did not come at the time I gave an alarm.'

Policeman Reuben Binns was the next witness called and, after relating the circumstances surrounding the fatality, he went on to tell the inquest that he had known Charlton for several years and as far as he was concerned, he did not bear the best of characters. PC Binns then shed some light on the relationship between Hannah

Samuel Charlton immediately following his vicious attack on Hannah.

Holroyd and Luke Normington. He was aware that a relationship had developed between the two prior to the murder, and he had witnessed Normington go in and out of the victim's house on several occasions. On the night of the murder, when he had heard the scream that alerted him to the crime, he had observed Normington running away from the scene. Normington later explained that he had fled the crime scene for fear that blame would be apportioned to him. In actual fact, at the time of the murder, Luke was drinking in the very same pub in which the inquest was being held, which was confirmed by David Naylor, landlord of the Second West Inn. He told the inquest, 'I know Luke Normington. He was in my house nearly all the evening, from something like six o'clock till one, but going out occasionally. He was in this house from twelve till ten minutes to one. He went about half past ten, and came in about half past eleven o'clock. He then stopped till ten minutes to one. He was rather "fresh" when he went out.'

Ellen Dyson, daughter of Samuel Charlton, was also called to give evidence. She told the inquest that her father lived with her, and on the night in question had left the house at about 8 p.m. to attend the teetotal meeting. Ellen knew about his relationship with Hannah Holroyd, which had commenced around Whitsuntide. Ellen, however, had no idea that the relationship had recently cooled, and thought that everything was fine between them. To her knowledge, her father had never expressed a wish to do the victim any harm.

The coroner then directed the jury's attention to the facts. He was in no doubt that there was sufficient evidence to send a person to trial and to hang him. Charlton was

Second West public house, Lidget Green.

left sitting with the woman at around a quarter to twelve, and about an hour afterwards, she was found in a pool of blood, with her throat cut. He was found to have left the house about the same time, to have gone to his own house and taken leave of his family. There was no doubt that if Charlton had been alive, he would have been sent to trial. The jury immediately returned a verdict of 'Wilful Murder against Samuel Charlton'.

Following the verdict, an inquest into the circumstances surrounding the death of Samuel Charlton was held at the same location. The coroner, Mr Dyson, once again presided, swearing in the following jury: Mr John Fearnsides, foreman, James Reaney, S. Settle, J. Denby, R. Collins, T. Bastow, Reuben Askwith, J. Willman, J. Clark, T. Pitt, E. Anderton, and James Halliwell. The coroner read the evidence that had been taken at the former inquest, telling the jury that a verdict of 'Wilful Murder' had been returned against Samuel Charlton, and that it was for them to determine whether the deceased Samuel Charlton had fallen by accident into the dam, or whether he had died from *felo de se* (self-murder, literally 'felon of himself').

John Knowles, a sergeant in the Bradford police force, was called first. He stated, 'I was on duty at Lidget Green on Monday night. I went to visit Reuben Binns on his beat at Lidget Green. When I was in Legrams Lane, I heard his signal – a double whistle – and I went back to him. I was between two and three hundred yards from him. He said there had been a murder on the Green. I went to the house of Hannah Holroyd. The woman was lying, weltering in blood, on the floor, with her throat cut, quite dead. I then went to Great Horton and called the surgeon, Mr Thomas.'

The sergeant then went on to describe the state of Charlton's body at the point he had been found. He said, 'He appeared quite fresh, as if he had not been long in the water. His clothes were correct, and there was no mark of injury upon him.' Charlton was well known to the officer, for he told the inquest that he had previously taken him in custody for felony, and more recently he had been committed for a month under the Worsted Act (fraud). He described Charlton as a dealer in cotton and waste, and not of good character. He had seen him repeatedly with Hannah Holroyd since last Whitsuntide, and known him to be in her house all night for several days a week since. The sergeant was convinced that Charlton was perfectly sound of mind, and had spoken to him as recently as the day before the murder.

The final witness, Henry Jowett, a police constable stationed at Great Horton, was then called and gave further evidence regarding Charlton's character. He said, 'I have known Charlton for thirty years. He was a man of bad character, and I believe he was a man of sound mind.'

The coroner then briefly directed the attention of the jury to the nature of the evidence, and asked them to consider whether or not the deceased was of sound mind. If they were of opinion that he was in a sound mind, their verdict would be *felo de se*. The jury then deliberated for a brief period and returned a verdict of *felo de se*.

The coroner said that he would have to give the constable a warrant ordering the body to be interred between the hours of nine and twelve the same night. In his twenty years as coroner, this was the first instance of *felo de se* that had occurred in more than 3,000 inquests in his district.

At the close of the inquest for Samuel Charlton, the constable, in accordance with the coroner's warrant, proceeded to make arrangements for the burial. The Act of Parliament required that a *felo de se* be interred within twenty-four hours of the inquest, and between the hours of 9 p.m. and 12 a.m. Accordingly, a grave was ordered to be dug in the burial ground attached to the Methodist chapel at Great Horton where his wife and other relatives had previously been interred. Around 11 p.m. the same night, the body was conveyed to Great Horton, under the direction of the relieving officer of the district. A crowd of more than 2,000 people had gathered in the road in front of the chapel yard. The angry mob met the coffin bearers at the gates as it was being taken from the hearse, and endeavoured to prevent the funeral from taking place. Such was the disgust that Charlton was to be buried among decent folk, the crowd were unrelenting, and exclamations such as 'throw it over the wall' and 'burn it' were mingled in the uproar. With the aid of the police, the coffin eventually reached the graveside, but then it was found that the grave was not deep enough, it being an old one. At record speed, the sextons proceeded to dig an alternative grave in a new plot. Meanwhile, one person addressed the crowd, expanding on the vicious character of the deceased and expressing regret that the annuals of Horton should be darkened with the record of a foul murder. The uproar from the angry mob carried on for most of the night, many of them remaining until 5 a.m. Once the grave had been dug, the burial was eventually completed, without the usual burial rites or a single mourner to shed a tear over his passing.

Wesleyan Methodist chapel, Great Horton Road.

Margaret Sutton (Gowland)
Double Murder and Suicide, 1860

Our quiet and orderly community has this week been thrown into great and unusual excitement by a tragedy unparalleled in atrocity in this district. Bradford, with its dense population, has happily been comparatively free from those fearful crimes against life which have characterised many large communities, and the occurrence of such a dreadful outrage now has excited feelings of intense horror and melancholy.

The murder in this instance is a double one, and the victims are the innocent offspring of a 'poor, unhappy frenzy stricken mother – loving not wisely, but too well', betrayed – if the chief witness at the inquest be not perjured – into the downward path of sin and shame, and then, ultimately, losing every ray of hope in the dark path on which she had entered, perpetrating the most horrible of all crimes as a fancied means of escape from irretrievable disgrace, degradation, and ruin.

For some months past, a woman of 34 years, named Margaret Sutton, has cohabited with a man of about 32 years of age, named John George Gowland, in a single furnished room on the ground floor, in Barkerend Road (formerly the High Street). They had two children – two pretty girls, were supposed to be married. This dreadful tragedy destroyed the illusion. His companion, under the heavy burden of mental anxiety, on Sunday night, cut the throats of her two children and her own, and the Gowland, the supposed husband, disowned the impeachment: he declared for the first time that they were not married and that jealousy alone had led the woman – his supposed wife – to destroy herself and her two children. The hope of marriage had been held out to her for several years, but, on various pleas, it was ever deferred. She at length doubted his fidelity, and her paramour returned home on Sunday night, to witness the result of the dreadful tragedy. Mrs Gowland (for as such she was known) was regarded in the neighbourhood as an amiable, gentle woman, and Gowland's allegations that she was only his mistress rest upon his unsupported testimony, the truth of which is doubted.

The Bradford Observer
Thursday 25 October 1860

The Murder

This chapter relates the circumstances that induced a mother to snuff out the lives of her precious young daughters before turning the blade on herself. Such was the shame of living over the brush with illegitimate children in Victorian Bradford that Margaret Sutton thought death a more favourable option. Certainly, her common law partner, John Gowland, was a shifty, immoral character. He was, however, not guilty of the murders, though he might as well have been, given the extreme hatred levelled towards him. That said, his apparent indifference to both his partner's suffering and the horrific destruction of his children did not help his cause one bit.

On Sunday 21 October 1860, John Gowland, having arrived at his home two hours before midnight, was somewhat puzzled to find the cottage in relative darkness with the door firmly locked. Knocking loudly on the door for some time, he failed to get the slightest response. After a brief interlude, he commenced knocking again, this time also calling out loudly to 'Margaret' to let him in. So loud was his knocking, it was inevitable that he would soon attract the attention of his neighbours, and presently Joshua Lee entered into some conversation regarding the inexplicable circumstances of Margaret's silence from the window of his bedroom. Taking into account that the family occupied

Church Bank, looking up towards Barkerend Road.

a single, furnished room on the ground floor and that Margaret very rarely went out, the pair was dumbfounded. After a short conversation, Joshua retired to his bed, leaving Gowland pacing quietly up and down the pavement smoking his pipe. After a while, he decided to knock the door once again. Listening carefully at the locked door, he was sure he could hear the faint sounds of movement within the cottage and proceeded to knock even harder, calling out to Margaret until he clearly heard the sound of a heavy object fall against the door from within. A short time later, the lock was slowly turned and the door swung open, admitting Gowland into the darkness. Taking a match from his pocket, which he quickly lit, he entered the room and glimpsed the sight of Margaret sat on bed before the match expired. With his hands shaking, he managed to light a second match while moving closer to the bedside, where he saw the full enormity of the dreadful scene. Margaret was sitting upright in the middle of the bed with her throat cut, the lifeless bodies of her dead children either side of her, also with their throats bleeding heavily. The bed and the floor were awash with blood. Such was his horror at the scene before him, he rushed out into the street seeking help from a neighbour living opposite called Edward Fawcett, who, witnessing the sickening sight, set forth at a pace to raise the alarm and inform the police. Within minutes, the small house was crowded with concerned neighbours, followed shortly by several police officers, including the Chief Constable Frederick William Grauhan, and at least two surgeons. The surgeons quickly tended to Margaret's wounds in an attempt to save her life, as it was clear that both Elizabeth Jane Gowland, aged four and a half, and Anne Gowland, aged just two, had long been dead. Their necks had been hacked by razors in such a way that even if they had been able to get medical attention prior to death, they would not have survived. Margaret, although very much incapacitated by her dreadful injuries, managed to make it known that she, and she alone, was responsible for the murders and not John Gowland. Pointing to a box, she made it clear to Gowland that she wanted him to see its contents, at the same time removing two letters from her pocket. The Chief Constable gave the box a cursory examination without apparently understanding what the poor woman was trying to say. Mr Grauhan and his constables then found documentation, including an order of affiliation in bastardy, of what she considered John Gowland's unfaithfulness to her and her children.

Margaret was taken by horse-drawn cab post-haste to the infirmary under a police guard, as the Chief Constable was justifiably concerned she might finish what she had started. Fearing she was about to die in any event, Margaret expressed her desire to make her peace, and the Revd J. Wade was summoned to her bedside, where he spent most of the night attempting to bring a little peace of mind to the tormented woman. Despite the surgeons believing Margaret was at death's door, she survived and was able to receive the Mayor Isaac Wright and his clerk early on the Monday morning, when she once again whispered her responsibility for the horrific crime. Although clearly guilty of murdering her young daughters in appalling circumstances, the Bradford townsfolk were extremely sympathetic towards Margaret and the dilemma that had induced her to destroy all that she loved, and instead directed their anger towards John George Gowland.

Isaac Wright, Mayor of Bradford from November 1859–November 1862. He visited Margaret the day after the murder.

Gowland was employed as an attorney's clerk by Messrs Terry and Watson, solicitors in the town, having arrived in Bradford some ten months earlier from the North East. His employment was certainly respectable enough and he had references, but the cottage Gowland shared with Margaret gave the impression of great poverty, with barely any furniture and just one bed shared by the whole family. When Gowland's employers heard of his immoral life after the tragedy, he was promptly dismissed.

The Investigation

On Tuesday 22 October 1860, the inquest for Elizabeth Jane Gowland opened before the coroner C. Jewison at the Boar's Head public house close by on Market Street. For the convenience of the jury, the coroner decided to inquire into the death of only one child, although the results would be the same in both cases. Mr Grauhan, the chief constable, stated that John Gowland refused to attend the inquest unless his expenses were paid and a cab sent for him. The coroner made it clear that, if that be the case, he would issue a warrant, which ultimately was not required as, by the time the jury had viewed the bodies of the children, Gowland had made his presence known to the coroner.

John George Gowland was then called and sworn in. He deposed,

I am an attorney's clerk. I reside in Bradford, Elizabeth Jane Gowland, the deceased, was my daughter. She was four years and six months old. I saw my daughter alive about ten minutes after six on Saturday night last. I saw her in my own house in Barkerend Road (formerly the High Street) about that time. Margaret Sutton is the name of the mother of the deceased. She was not my wife. I left her there and also Elizabeth Jane Gowland and Anne Gowland, the daughters of the deceased. I returned about ten o'clock the same night. I knocked at the door, but received no answer. I knocked for about five minutes, and received no answer. Mr Joshua Lee, who resides at the next door, then opened his chamber window and said, 'Your wife can't be in.' I replied that it was strange: I never found her out before at that time. I then asked him if he had any idea where she was, and he stated that he had not. I then charged my pipe and began to smoke in the street in front of the house. After smoking for twenty minutes I knocked at the door again. I then heard a slight noise. I immediately began to repeat my knocking. I then heard more noise, and called out, 'Margaret, Margaret.' I then heard more noise. I repeated my knocking, and cried out in the same manner, being satisfied that there was someone inside; and then I heard a noise as if something was thrown against the door. I again repeated my knocking and called out in the same manner as before, 'Margaret, honey! Why don't you open the door?' About a minute afterwards, the door was opened and the lock was unturned. I went about two yards within, and, finding all in darkness, I took a match out of my pocket, and lighted it. I then advanced a yard further and saw her sitting upon the bed. The match was finished and I then lighted another match. I then perceived that her throat was cut and the bed clothes all saturated with blood.

I also perceived the eldest daughter lying in bed, full dressed, on the right hand side of her, and the youngest on the left side. I then said to her, 'Good heavens! Margaret, you have murdered the innocent children!' She made no reply. I then rushed out of the house immediately, and ran across to a neighbour, named Edward Fawcett, who resides opposite. I saw Fawcett, and I said to him, 'Oh! Good heavens! Come with me; there is murder in my house.' He then replied and said, 'Murder!' He then came with me to my house. We both looked in and he immediately ran out. We both looked and found both the children, Elizabeth Jane and Anne Gowland, were dead. Margaret Sutton was sitting up in bed. There seemed to be a deep cut wound in front of the neck of Margaret. Fawcett and I immediately ran out – we rushed out quickly. He used some expression which I don't recollect. I then called out to Joshua Lee, and shouted 'murder.' A great number of people now assembled. We went into the house, and I asked someone to go for a doctor. Two or three doctors immediately came. The chief constable and several police men came. Margaret Sutton beckoned to me, and I went to her. She then gave me two keys. She motioned to a box. I opened the large box to which she pointed. Some person stated that very likely there would be a written paper found in the box which would state why the deed had been done. I replied that it could not be, because she could neither read nor write. I did not find any writing in the box. I took 8s out of the box, and I believe I then locked it. This was all the money I saw. I did not look a minute there. I was then told she wanted me, and I went to the bed side and said 'There is no writing,' and she then took two letters from her pocket. The first letter I saw was directed by myself to her brother at Hylton, and the second was one received from him.

The letters were produced by Inspector Shuttleworth, and the Coroner read on, as follows:

Hylton. Oct. 19
Dear Maggie,
In reply to your letter, I am very sorry to hear of the situation you are placed in, but you have no one to blame but yourself, as I and your sister Ann advised you not to go with him, but it was all to no use – you would have your own way. I thought you had plenty of him before, when you left him twice, and went to him again. Mrs Laing said she tried all she could to keep you away from him, but it was all of no avail, and she will never look to you again. Mrs Laing met your mother at Sunderland and asked her if you had got a situation. I, herself, and Mr Jas Laing signed our names to you and Gowland. She was very anxious to know, and I wrote to Gowland and I enclose his reply, for I do not think you know anything about it.

Dear Maggie,
I think you had better stay with your husband and not leave him a third time. You know sister Mary is not here to mind the children now. You will only set people on to talking about you again. If you cannot live with him, you can get law to make him keep you and the children. I remain, your affectionate brother,
W. M. RICHARDSON

Gowland continued:

> Someone then said, 'Who has done the deed?' and she put up her hand, and motioned towards herself. I had had no reason to think she would do anything to harm herself. She was a nice gentle creature. About a fortnight ago, she intimated to me that she would like to be married. I replied that I would be married before the year was ended, and I told her further that it would have been done in the North of England, but we were afraid of its being known there. I received letters morning after morning from various parts, and she seemed to scrutinise the letters very much. One morning, about ten or twelve days ago, I asked what were her reasons for examining the letters so closely, and she replied. 'Well, you know, Gowland, I have a good right to be jealous of you.' I then asked her why, and she replied, 'Have I not been told you have been seen talking to women?' I then told her that as a person in my capacity of life, as a law clerk, I was bound to do so in the way of giving advice on behalf of my governors. She occasionally asked me who the letters were from, and I told her on every occasion. I also tendered the letters to her and told her she might take them to a neighbour and get them read.

Mr Grauhan asked the witness if he had been seen in a brothel recently. Gowland, after some hesitation said:

> About a fortnight ago I went to a house of ill fame opposite to speak as to its being an improper house, and to tell them I should lodge a complaint against them to the magistrates for keeping an improper house. I paid for some oysters. Margaret came in at the time and said, 'What are you doing here?' and I said, 'Well come along with me, and I will tell you.' I told her what I had been threatening them with proceedings. I did not tell her that I had been treating anybody with oysters. I treated nobody in particular, but I was ready to treat anybody. The man's wife asked me to stand treat, and I treated everybody around. I did not treat any person in the house in particular. I can't say whether I told Margaret that. I am under the impression she has been jealous of late. She was perfectly satisfied with what I told her at the time. She has always been kind. I deny that we have been parted twice; we have been parted only once. I believe this dreadful affair has been the result of jealousy, and that feeling may have affected her mind.

The coroner then explained to the jury that the actions of Margaret Sutton were not justified as a consequence of any act of Gowland. Whatever his conduct, this did not make him responsible for the crime. No doubt he might be severely blamed by the public, and properly so, but he was, he said, ready to answer any question, and the jury could now put any question they chose. Several of the jury continued to ask questions, and Gowland stated that he received a pound a week from his employers, but he received money besides, and he never allowed Margaret less than 18s per week.

Joshua Lee was then called, followed by Edward Fawcett, who both corroborated Gowland's account. A further witness, Ruth Gell, was then sworn in. She said:

1855.   Marriage solemnized at the Parish Church of St. Oswald, in or near the City of Durham.

No.	When Married	Names and Surnames.	Age.	Condition.	Rank or Profession.	Residence.	Father's Name and Surname	Rank or Profession.
139	1855. 23 Sept.	John Geo. Gowland.	25	Bachelor.	Attorney's Clerk.	Bishop Wearmouth Sunderland	Dead.	None.
		Margaret Sutton.	26	Spinster.				

Married at the Parish Church according to the rites and ceremonies of the Established Church, by license by me,   HENRY THOMAS FOX.

This marriage was solemnized between us,   JOHN GEORGE GOWLAND,

Her

MARGARET ✗ SUTTON.

Mark.

In the presence of us,   ELIZABETH PROUD,

HENRY WILKINSON.

The above is a true copy of the particulars contained in the register belonging to the parish of St. Oswald, respecting the marriage of John George Gowland and Margaret Sutton, on the 23rd day of September, 1855.   HENRY THOMAS FOX.

The supposed marriage certificate of John and Margaret Gowland.

My husband is Alfred Gell and he is a leather currier. As I was going from my own door, on Sunday night, Edward Fawcett was running down the street, greatly alarmed. I was going from my own door into the house. I heard a knocking, and was told there was something to do in Gowland's and went in. I went to the bedside and saw Mrs Gowland herself and two children had all their throats cut. I said, 'Mrs. Gowland, who has done this?' and she put her hand out and pointed to a bloody razor on the bed, and then pointed to her bosom. She did not speak, but only motioned so as to make me understand it was her.

George Priestley Smith, surgeon, High Street, was then sworn in. He said:

I was sent for to see Mrs Gowland and her two children about half past ten on Sunday night. I was not aware till now that her name is Margaret Sutton, and not Margaret Gowland. I went to her house and found her sitting on the bed with her throat cut, and her children with their throats cut at the head of the bed. The skin, muscles and windpipe were all cut through and divided; the artery and jugular vein were not injured. The bleeding had completely ceased when I got there, at near eleven o'clock. Her face and arms were covered with blood. She was quite conscious, but whispered very indistinctly. The two children were lying quite dead, behind her, at the head of the bed. They were both on their right sides with their throats cut. She made a motion as if she wanted to say something to me, and she motioned as if she wished me to understand she had done it herself. This razor I found behind her upon the bed. The wounds in the throats of the children were deep wounds. I have no doubt that the death was caused by these wounds in the throat.

The coroner then suggested that a post-mortem examination should be made and adjourned until 6 November. As the jury left, Gowland began to complain of the inconvenience of an adjournment, if he was required to attend. While claiming great affection for Margaret Sutton, he said he felt he was in danger in the town, and wished to depart it as soon as possible. The coroner immediately bound him in his own recognisance to appear on 6 November.

Shortly after the inquest was adjourned, John Gowland was arrested and placed in the lock-up. The following morning, he was brought to the Borough Court before Mr Alderman Brown and Mr Alderman Rand. A large crowd followed the prisoner as he passed through the streets going to and from his cell.

On Gowland being called into the dock, Mr Grauhan, the chief constable, stated that he held in his hand a document that purported to be a copy of the register of the marriage of John George Gowland to Margaret Sutton, at the parish church of St Oswald, in or near the city of Durham. He (the prisoner) was present as a witness at the inquest held on his two children the previous day, and there he swore that he was not married to Margaret Sutton, who had lived with him as his wife, and who was now in the infirmary. Mr Grauhan stated that the document had been found among other papers in the possession of the prisoner. He (Mr Grauhan) had already written to the incumbent of St Oswald in Durham, and he now asked the magistrates to remand Gowland until Monday next. He thought he should be able to show that

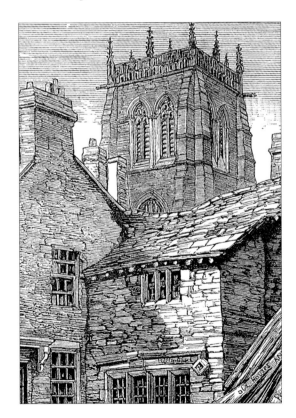

Old houses and the parish church, 1882.

the prisoner had made use of this document while in Bradford and that, if he were not guilty of perjury, he was guilty of forgery. Gowland was then sent into the dock, where he asked to be bailed. Mr Grauhan objected to the application, believing that the prisoner was of a most immoral character and that in all probability he would leave Bradford immediately. The application for bail was thus refused and Mr Alderman Brown ordered the prisoner to be remanded to the cells. Gowland's demeanour after the hearing was said to indicate the most callous indifference to his position and the suffering of his family.

Later that afternoon, Chief Constable Grauhan asked Margaret at the infirmary if she was married to Gowland, and she replied that she was not. Mr Grauhan, at the suggestion of the coroner, then formally charged her with the crime of murdering her two children, with the usual caution that she need not say anything unless she chose, and that, if she did say anything, it would be taken down and might be used as evidence against her elsewhere. She offered no reply. That very same afternoon, the funeral of the children took place at Scholemoor Cemetery, Necropolis Road. The funeral procession at the rear of the hearse was made up of little children who had been the playmates of the deceased. A large crowd of mainly women followed, many in tears. At the graveside, the funeral service was read in a solemn manner by the Revd W. Mundy, curate of Great Horton.

On 1 November, the *Bradford Observer* printed the following article, which proved that the marriage certificate was a forgery:

THE MURDER OF TWO CHILDREN

On Thursday last, Mr. Grauhan, the chief constable, received a letter from the vicar of St Oswald, Durham, in which the Revd Gentleman stated that he carefully searched the register of marriage in the parish of St Oswald, for the year 1855, and found no entry of the solemnization of any marriage between John George Gowland and Margaret Sutton during that year. He added that there could be no doubt that the certificate described was a forgery. In answer to another letter then written by Mr Grauhan, the vicar of St Oswald replied that to the best of his knowledge and belief, there neither was nor had there been during his incumbency any clergyman of the name of Henry Thomas Fox, resident in the parish of St Oswald. The certificate of the entry sent him, he added, was not worded in the form uniformly adopted by him or his officials. Mr. Grauhan also received by the same post a letter from the brother of Margaret Sutton, Mr Richardson, of Hylton, Durham, in which he enclosed copies of two letters, which he stated he had received from his sister. They were as follows:

Dear Brother,
With heartfelt grief I write these few lines to you to inform you of the situation I am now placed in. I am not in a house of my own at present, not am I likely to be, the way as my husband is going on-the same as he was in Sunderland, if anything worse. I really cannot bear it any longer. Dear Brother, if I am spared till Monday, I intend to leave him, so that you may expect me by that time, if I can get sufficient money of him on the Saturday to bring me and the children home unknown to him,

The Old Courthouse, Westgate.

as he will not let me come if he knows. Please not to say anything about it till you
see me, perhaps he might get to know. I shall come by the Great Northern (North
Eastern) but it will not be until night; so you will be there to meet me. Dear Brother,
in haste, from me,
Your unhappy sister,
MARGARET GOWLAND, Bradford
Please write to me by Sunday, and send it in the envelope directed for Mrs
Hutchinson; then he will not know about it, and I will get the letter forwarded to
me Good bye.

Bradford, Oct. 21
Dear Brother,
Let the consequences be as it may, I shall leave Gowland tomorrow, Monday, I
cannot put up with his treatment of me any longer. So you may expect to me to come
tomorrow night by the last train to Aylton.
MARGARET GOWLAND

On Monday 28 October, John George Gowland was again brought to the Borough
Court. The magistrates present were the mayor (Isaac Wright, Esq.), W. B. Addison,
Esq., John Hollings, Esq., Wm. Rand, Esq., Mr Alderman Light, and Mr Alderman

Brown. The court was densely crowded with spectators. The passages leading to the court, as well as the streets outside, were crowded with people anxious to obtain a sight of the prisoner.

Frederick William Grauhan, the chief constable, stated that the prisoner was remanded last Wednesday. He (Mr Grauhan) wrote to the Revd Edward Sneyd, the vicar of St Oswald, Durham, to ascertain whether such persons had ever been married at St Oswald parish in 1855, a document purporting to be a certified copy of the prisoner's marriage with the woman having been found among his papers. The Revd E. Sneyd wrote to say that he could not find anything to suggest that any such marriage had taken place. The name of the clergyman purporting to have signed the supposed certificate was Henry Thomas Fox. There was no clergyman there of that name.

'This certificate is in the handwriting of the prisoner. I cannot, however, prove that he used it for a fraudulent purpose. The charge of perjury, therefore, cannot be sustained, nor can the charge of forgery.' The magistrates consulted for a few minutes, and the mayor said that the prisoner was discharged.

Bradford High Street, viewed from the churchyard.

Gowland was then moved to the area below the courthouse, as it was not safe for him to leave as a large, angry crowd was waiting for him outside the courthouse. Gowland remained there for five hours, until it was at last deemed safe for the officers to help him escape over the high wall in the rear of the courthouse into Drake Street. By now the whole country was aware of the tragedy, which had created much sympathy for Margaret. The *Durham Chronicle* printed the following article, which shed some light upon Gowland's character:

The prisoner Gowland is a native of Durham, his mother and other relatives now living in the town. The case has consequently excited a great deal of attention here; and sincere sympathy is expressed for the unfortunate woman he had induced to become his victim, and who, when heartbroken by his cruelty, dared to take the lives of her children and of herself. Gowland himself is a well-known person, as he was somewhat of 'a character'. He was formerly an attorney's clerk in the employment of Mr Henry John Marshall, in this city, and was afterwards similarly employed in Sunderland. He is a vulgar, impudent, conceited fellow and it is somewhat surprising the influence he seems to have acquired over some of his female acquaintances. He was committed to Durham prison by the Sunderland bench, of magistrates, on the 23rd March last, on a charge of stealing household goods, the property of John Cuthbertson Bellas, at Sunderland. He had been living in adultery with Mrs Bellas at lodgings, whilst the prosecutor, a sailor, was at sea, and for this offence he was sentenced by the Court of Quarter Sessions to six months' imprisonment. He also appeared before the magistrates at the Newcastle police court for assaulting a woman whom he had taken to his lodgings, by pitching her out of the window.

Whilst at Sunderland he induced a number of silly people to subscribe one shilling a week each to him for the purpose, as he induced them to believe, of carrying on proceedings for the recovery of some landed estates in this neighbourhood, to which he pretended he had a title. This swindle would have probably been exposed at the time, but it happened that he was sent to gaol from Sunderland before the poor people discovered they were being duped.

On Thursday 8 November 1860, the *Bradford Observer* reported on the death of Margaret Sutton and the anguish she suffered in her final days:

THE RECENT TRAGEDY IN HIGH STREET
DEATH OF MRS GOWLAND

At a few minutes past six o'clock on Friday morning 2 November, Margaret Gowland alias Sutton died in the Infirmary. Her demise, as we stated in our last, was imminent, and from Thursday evening she gradually sank. The highest medical skill and the most unremitting attention and kindness were exerted in vain. Up to Thursday, she was apparently frequently disturbed by severe mental agony. She frequently talked of her children and uttered the wish that she were with them! On Thursday she appeared to find consolation in listening to the reading of portions of Scripture in which there was the promise of forgiveness to the penitent in heart, and when the reader ceased, she desired to read the passages again. In the evening she became more calm and quiet. About one o'clock on Friday morning she remarked that 'she was now reconciled,' and 'she hoped God would forgive her.' From that time, though sensible nearly to the close of her life, she sank rather rapidly, and at length she passed peacefully away.

At Margaret's inquest, which was held at the Boar's Head Hotel before the coroner C. Jewison, the jury agreed to return the following verdict: 'That the deceased, Margaret Sutton, died from the effects of a wound on her throat, inflicted by herself with a razor, she being at the time in a state of temporary derangement of mind.' The jury also delivered the following verdicts upon Elizabeth Jane Gowland and Anne Gowland that they were killed or murdered by their mother, and that she did this at a time when she was labouring under temporary insanity of mind. Following the verdicts, John Gowland was waiting in an adjoining room to receive his wages for two days' attendance as a witness. On leaving the Boar's Head, he was surrounded by a group of women who had gathered there. Some of them jostled him in a rough manner. Taking to his heels he was pursued by the crowd through Hustler Gate. At Sun Bridge he took refuge in a cab, and drove off beyond the reach of the maddening crowd. The following day Gowland was observed in Barkerend (High Street). A mob of men and boys quickly gathered, some of whom began to attack him and once again he made good his escape. Gowland departed Bradford the same night catching the train at the Midland Station at 9.50 p.m. where a crowd had gathered and it was only with the assistance of the police that Gowland was able to leave Bradford in one piece.

This was not to be the last to be heard of John George Gowland, as can be seen below:

DURHAM MIDSUMMER SESSION

JOHN GEORGE GOWLAND (43), Law clerk and accountant, was found guilty of having obtained the sum of 10s, with intention to defraud Robert Trusty, at Durham, on 10th April. The prosecutor met the prisoner at Durham on the day in question, and asked advice respecting some legal proceedings. The prisoner represented himself to be a Solicitor, and on that representation he was entrusted to attend to the affairs of the prosecutor, who paid him fees to the amount of 10s. The prisoner, against whom a previous conviction for felony was put in, was sentenced to twelve months' imprisonment.

The Newcastle Courant
Friday 3 July 1868

The funeral of Margaret Sutton took place at Scholemoor Cemetery on the afternoon of 5 November 1860. The cortège consisted of three cabs, in which the sister of the deceased and a number of neighbours, attired in mourning, followed the hearse as it departed from the infirmary grounds, soon after two o'clock. A large number of people, principally women, were gathered in the adjoining streets, and they followed the funeral procession as it departed. The crowd increased as the procession made its way to the cemetery, numbering some 2–3,000 people. The Revd J. Wade, the curate of the parish church, officiated. Having attended to Margaret in the last days of her life, he performed the final office over her grave, reading the sublime and touching burial service of the Church of England with great solemnity. The grave is situated near the western boundary of the cemetery and was regarded as a superior plot, the cost of which was paid by the general public. The coffin was deposited in the grave, and the remains of the children were afterwards placed in the same one, having been removed from a plot in another part of the cemetery. The bottom of the grave was built round with bricks and covered with flags.

Margaret left written directions as to the manner in which Mr Grauhan, the chief constable, should dispose of property she left behind, which included 20s, a quantity of clothes, a Bible, and a wedding ring. Her mother, Elizabeth Sutton, of South Hylton, Sunderland; a younger sister, also residing at Sunderland; and a sister of Gowland (a Mrs Dixon, residing at Undercliffe Cemetery lodge), were the legatees.

The beautifully carved headstone, which depicts Margaret and her daughters and paid for by public subscription, can still be found today nestling peacefully under a tree at Scholemoor Cemetery. Despite the passage of 153 years, the headstone stands tall and prominent as a testament to the compassion and sorrow felt by thousands of people in Victorian Bradford for Margaret and her little girls.

The grave of Margaret Sutton.

Francis William Neale
Wife Murder, 1888

A SINGULAR AFFAIR IN BRADFORD
A WOMAN FOUND DEAD – ARREST OF THE HUSBAND

A mysterious and painful affair occurred in Bradford on Friday night, resulting in the death of a woman, and the arrest of her husband on suspicion of being the cause of her decease. The woman's name was Mrs Neale, and her husband, who is now in custody, is Francis William Neale. The parties carried on the business of stay makers and ladies' under clothing providers at No. 14, Darley Street, their private residence being at No. 11, Grosvenor Terrace, Belle Vue, Manningham. It appears that for ten or a dozen years past Mr and Mrs Neale have led an uncomfortable life, Mrs Neale having been addicted to habits of intemperance.

Bradford Daily Telegraph
2 June 1888

The Murder

Francis (William) and Etty (Esther) Neale had been married for about nineteen years prior to her untimely death. The couple had three sons; the eldest, Willie (William), was fourteen years old in 1888. Both Francis and Esther came from respectable families. Francis, who was originally from Martham, Norfolk, had moved to Leeds many years prior, gaining employment in a hosiery shop. Later he joined Messrs J. Holmes & Co., Darley Street, where he met Esther, who was two years his junior. When the couple got married in September 1869, they took over the business, which, at that time, was well established by her mother, Mrs Smith. Before her marriage, Esther Smith was considered to be a highly respectable and well thought of young woman. The marriage, however, proved disastrous. Although they were both fond of drink, Esther was more so. In the weeks leading up to her death, she had been drunk most days and had taken to staying out overnight without offering any explanation.

When Esther was discovered dead after a severe beating, no one was particularly surprised, nor were they shocked that blame was pointed firmly in the direction of her husband. The couple had spent the previous twelve years of their married life fighting like cat and dog in abject misery. Their drunken arguments were part of

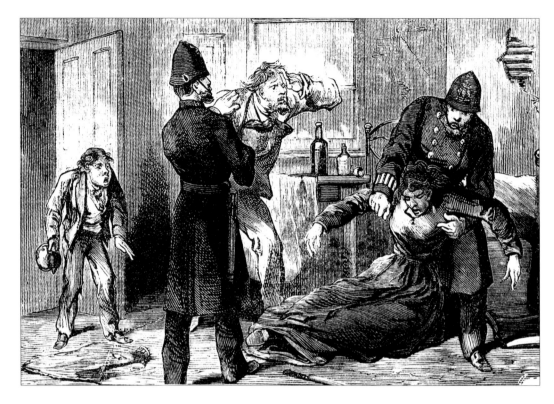

A contemporary illustration depicting the crime scene.

everyday life and almost legendary in the Manningham district. Only three days prior to her suspicious death, PC Dunn from the free library had chanced upon Mrs Neale screaming 'murder', and after investigating the call of distress he had witnessed Francis Neale standing over his wife menacingly while apparently threatening to put a 'shutter bolt' through her. Given the circumstances, one might think it a foregone conclusion that justice would have been both swift and fair, but then we are forgetting this was Victorian England, where people were judged primarily on their morals. For despite the fact Francis Neale had clearly kicked his wife to death, breaking five ribs in a drunken and jealous frenzy, Esther Neale was, in the words of the coroner, 'guilty of the greatest indecency it was possible for any woman to be guilty of.'

The first indication that Esther had come to any harm was at around 10.40 p.m. on Friday 1 June when John Cockcroft, landlord of the Airedale public house at Otley Road, was told in the commercial room by an excited and distressed Francis Neale that he believed his wife Etty was dead. John asked Neale exactly what he meant, to which he replied, 'I cannot move her'. Mr Cockcroft, Esther's cousin, asked Neale if a doctor had been informed. Neale replied in the negative. The two men immediately left the public house – Neale went in search of the doctor and Cockcroft in the direction of the draper's shop in Darley Street. As Cockcroft walked along Kirkgate, he met PC Gibbons and PC Parsons and made them aware of the situation. Together, the three men went to investigate the possibility that a death had occurred.

Arriving at the shop, John Cockcroft made his way up to the attic where, to his horror, he discovered his relative lying dead on the floor. PC Gibbons then entered the room, followed by PC Parsons. By the state of the furniture that had been thrown about, they deduced that this had been the scene of a fight or argument. About 2 feet from the door, they observed the lifeless form of a woman stretched out on the floor with an overcoat placed loosely over her torso. Her body still felt warm, indicating that she had died recently. It was also evident that after her death, her body had been moved to the position where it was found. The constables, on removing the coat, found Esther semi-naked, wearing just a chemise, a red cloth bodice, boots and stockings. Her head was resting on a jacket, and her mouth was bleeding. Constable Parsons also detected some blood on the floor near to the window, along with parts of a broken clay pipe, and a quantity of glass from a broken window. He looked for the dead woman's outer clothing, but couldn't find any except for what was already on her body. Afterwards, however, the constables located some clothing in the back yard, along with Neale's hat, which had evidently been thrown out of the broken window.

Around fifteen minutes later, Francis Neale entered the room, trembling and agitated. John Cockcroft asked him if he had sent for a doctor, to which he replied, 'I have been to Dr Tacey's, and he could not come, and he told me to go to Dr Taylor's, but I didn't go.' Unsatisfied with Neale's response, Cockcroft questioned him further as to how Esther had got into this state. Neale replied that he left the shop at a quarter to six, leaving his wife and the female assistant there. He returned shortly before eight o'clock, and found his wife intoxicated. Being unable to get her to go home, he then left her and went drinking himself. A little later he returned, only to find his wife in the company of the man Black. At that time, he stated, Etty was upstairs in the back room, naked but for her boots. Mr Black was standing by Etty with his hand on her shoulder. He had a struggle with Black and succeeded in turning him out of the shop. He left his wife upstairs, who was still intoxicated, and went to the White Lion and Blake's, where he had some drink, and shortly after ten o'clock he returned to the shop once again. This time, he found the woman lying on the floor in the back room in an unconscious state. Blood was oozing from her mouth, leading him to believe that she had suffered a fit. Without doing anything apart from sponging her mouth, he had then rushed to the Airedale Inn to inform Mr Cockcroft. Constable Parsons, after hearing Neale's explanation, charged him with causing the death of his wife. To this, Neale replied, 'I have not touched her.' The officer then told him that he would take him down to the town hall, and requested Cockcroft to accompany them. When taken into custody, Neale was still slightly drunk but fully aware of the gravity of the situation.

Samuel Lodge, the police surgeon, examined the body at the crime scene, which revealed several bruises (the result of either blows or kicks) and a slight wound on the back of the head. One of Etty's arms was also bruised, as was one thigh. From this superficial examination, the police were unsure if the injuries were caused by violence or if they were sufficiently serious to have caused her death. Dr Lodge then ordered the body to be sent to the mortuary for a post-mortem, which was carried out by the police.

James Withers, chief constable of Bradford, November 1874–October 1894.

At that point, the case was one of suspicion rather than a true allegation against Francis Neale. The investigators, knowing Neale and Black had been fighting, did not know if Esther had got involved in the struggle and obtained the injuries as a result, which then may or may not have led to her death. Another possibility was that during the excitement of her husband catching her naked with Mr Black, she suffered a fatal fit.

During the night, Neale was closely watched in his cell, where he appeared quiet and very depressed. The following morning, as large crowds gathered around the draper's shop where the death had occurred, Francis Neale was formally charged with causing the death of his wife by Superintendent Campbell at the town hall, in light of further medical evidence from Dr Lodge. The prisoner, now completely sober, gave a much fuller account of his wife's death than he had when he was first arrested, but made no mention of assaulting her.

Throughout the whole investigation, Neale never once admitted to causing the death of his wife, though this was clearly not the case, as can be seen in the following enquiries.

The Investigation

NEALE BEFORE THE MAGISTRATES' COURT

On Saturday 2 June at Bradford Borough Police Court before the mayor (Ald. J. L. Morley), Ald. F. Priestman, Mr Arthur Briggs, and Mr J. Ambler, Francis William Neale, aged 41 and employed as a draper, of Grosvenor Terrace, Bradford, brought before the magistrates on a charge of causing the death of his wife, Esther Neale, aged 39.

Superintendent Campbell told the court that the prisoner had been apprehended on a charge of causing the death of his wife last night. His wife was found laid dead in the house or shop in Darley Street, under very suspicious circumstances, and he (Mr Campbell) asked the court for a remand until after the inquest, which had been fixed for Monday.

Detective-Inspector Dobson was called and stated that he had formally charged the prisoner Neale with causing the death of his wife that morning, and in reply the prisoner had said, 'I went to the shop in Darley Street about nine o'clock last night, and found my wife with Mr Black in the back room. My wife was naked, except that she had her boots and stockings on. Her stockings were down. I said to Black 'Now you b——d villain, I've caught you,' and I picked up the sweeping brush and tried to strike him with it, but he pushed it away, and rushed downstairs. I went after him, but he got away. I went back to the shop and then found my wife in the room with her chemise on. She was tipsy. I left her seated on a box near the window breathing very heavily. When I came back she was laid on the floor, and I lifted her up and put something under her head and was going to leave. She was heavy and deathlike, and as there was no one else near I went to her cousin's at the Airedale Hotel, and afterwards went back to the shop, and then for Dr Tacey.

Mr Freeman, who represented the prisoner, said that his client could give a thorough explanation about the whole affair.

The Mayor: The prisoner will be remanded until Tuesday next.

THE INQUEST

On Monday 4 June, the Bradford Borough Coroner (Mr J. G. Hutchinson) opened the inquiry at the Town Hall respecting the death of Esther Neale, wife of William Francis Neale, Draper, Darley Street, Bradford, whose death took place on Friday 1 June 1888.

The Chief Constable (Mr James Withers) was present on behalf of the police; Mr A. Neill Messrs Neill and Broadbent) appeared for the prisoner Neale; Mr J. Freeman, represented Mr Black; and Mr C. L. Atkinson watched the proceedings on behalf of Mrs Smith, the mother of the deceased woman.

Maria Bentley, 34, Bower Street, was the first witness called. She stated that she was an assistant in the employment of Francis Wm. Neale, the husband of the deceased, at the shop No. 14, Darley Street. She had been in Mr Neale's service about five years, and knew the deceased, who assisted in the shop. On Friday last she went to business about nine o'clock in the morning, and the deceased came about eleven o'clock. About one o'clock, witness went to dinner, leaving Mrs Neale in charge of the premises. She returned about a quarter past two, at which time there was no-one in the shop, but as she walked to the further end of the place, Mr Neale entered from upstairs and said, 'Mrs Neale has gone out, and I have sent Alex (his son) to see where she goes. They have eaten all the chops. I will go out to dinner.' He then left the shop, and returned between a quarter and half-past three. He asked, 'Has Mrs Neale or Alex come back?' and on being told 'no' he went upstairs. Whilst he was there at about a quarter to four Mrs Neale returned, drunk. Witness looked at her, and the deceased, observing this, said, 'You need not look at me,' went behind the counter and sat on a buffet. Mr Neale then entered the shop and said 'Oh! Then you have come back.' She replied, 'Yes,' and leaning over the counter towards her husband said, 'Will you go upstairs and wash yourself; you look dirty.' She declined, saying, 'No, I shan't; I'm as clean as you.' 'Then do as you like,' he replied, and walked out of the shop. Mrs Neale looked white, and on witness asking if she was ill, she replied 'Yes, my head's very bad.' After having a cup of tea the deceased went upstairs, declining the assistance of witness in ascending the steps. Mr Neale returned about five o'clock and joined his wife upstairs. On entering the room he said 'Willie, get up and let me have my tea,' but the deceased objected saying, 'Let the boy finish his tea; he has worked hard enough to-day.' As witness had finished her tea she rose and said, 'Willie can have my chair,' then went down into the shop. On the way she heard Mrs Neale say, 'Oh, yes, go, and let him have his tea.' Quarrelling then ensued for about ten minutes, and then the husband entered the shop and asked, 'Have you had a customer in?' and on being informed in the affirmative said, 'Then I'll take the money,' took it, and left the premises, and witness did not see him again that day. Shortly after she went upstairs to dress the deceased's hair, and whilst doing so Mrs Neale made a complaint. In consequence of this, witness felt at the right side of her mistress's head, and there found a large lump. After this she made a further complaint. After this Mrs Neale went into the shop and stayed till nearly seven o'clock, when Mr Black entered. He asked 'Is Mr Neale in,' and Mrs Neale said 'No, but I expect him in a few minutes, and I'll ask him to wait, but perhaps you'll wait?' He remained in the shop and conversed with her (witness) about her holidays. She left about five minutes past seven o'clock, leaving Mrs Neale, Black and Willie in the shop. When the deceased came in the morning to the shop she did not appear to be exactly sober, but when she (witness) left her in the evening she looked a good deal better. Witness did not again see the deceased alive. The deceased and her husband had had frequent quarrels recently; they had scarcely done anything else for the last two months. She had seen Neale strike the deceased more than once, but not lately. She could not say how many times, nor when.

Mr Neill (defence) commented: generally the deceased had been addicted to drink during the whole time she had been in her employment. She frequently got drunk. When she was in drink she was very quarrelsome, and she had seen her push Mr Neale out of the shop door, but had not seen her strike him, nor had she seen her throw things at him.

Mr Neill asked the witness: For several weeks before that was she ever sober? – I don't think she was. She was drunk every day. On Monday and Tuesday she was not ill from the effects of drink? – I dare say she was. She was ill.

Witness, in answer to further questions, said that on the Wednesday, Thursday, and Friday the deceased was the worse for drink, and she was the worse for drink on the Friday at four o'clock. She did not know whether there had been any dinner

Darley Street, Bradford.

prepared for the husband that day. Within the last few weeks witness had heard quarrels between the deceased and her husband, when he complained of her not going home at night, and not accounting for where she had been all night. She had heard the husband complain about this at least half a dozen times during the last three or four weeks.

William Neale said he was a son of the deceased, and was employed at the shop in Darley Street. On Friday last he was at his father's shop between eleven and twelve o'clock in one of the upper rooms with his mother. She was then under the influence of drink. His father came into the room, and as witness was clearing out the cupboard there was a quarrel about it. He was there about five o'clock the same afternoon with his mother. His father then came in for his tea, and said to witness, 'Get up and let me get my tea,' to which his mother replied, 'No, let him finish his tea, he has worked hard enough.' After this there was there was a quarrel about the dinner, in the course of which his father knocked his mother's head against a recess. In doing so he got hold of her head with both hands, and knocked it against the wall, and at the same time called her a liar. She complained about him not having left her any dinner the day before, and it was for this that he called her a liar. When he did this his mother screamed and began to cry. His father then went downstairs, and soon after left the premises. Shortly before seven o'clock Mr Black entered the shop and enquired for Mr Neale. Accepting an invitation of the deceased Mr Black remained. Miss Bentley left about five minutes past seven, and about ten minutes after his mother sent him for some soap. He fetched the soap, and on returning found his mother and Mr Black still in the shop. Witness then told his mother they required some soap for home, whereupon she gave him 3d, and he went for it and then proceeded home, leaving Mr Black and the deceased still in the shop. He did not again see his mother alive; nor did he again see his father that day. On several occasions during the past fortnight he had seen his father strike his mother.

John Black, concrete floor layer, of 47, Carlisle Terrace, Manningham, being called said, 'I have known the deceased about eighteen months, and her husband about four years. I have done business with her husband, and have been in the habit of calling at his shop in Darley Street in a friendly way. On Friday last I called about a quarter past seven and saw the deceased, Miss Bentley and Willie Neale. I asked for Mr Neale. Mrs Neale said, "Come in, Mr Black; he had gone out and will be back in a few minutes." Miss Bentley was dressing to leave business for the day, and about three customers came while she was doing so. I conversed with the deceased on family and business matters. I remember the deceased sending Willie for some soap, and after he had gone home the deceased asked me to assist her to close the shop, and I did so. Before this a customer had entered the shop, and desiring the approval of her mother to the goods asked Mrs Neale to keep the shop open a little longer. The deceased consented to do so, and I was about to go and bid her good night. She, however, asked me to stay, and I did so until the young lady returned and took the goods of which she had approved. The young lady returned about a quarter past eight, and it was after this that I consented to assist in closing the front door of the premises. Mrs Neale then retired to the back part of the shop, saying she would go for her keys, hat, bag, and other articles, and would walk home with me. I remained in the shop for some time, but she did not come, and I called out to her twice, and she replied each time, "I am coming." Still she did not come down, and I next heard her call out "Come up, I want you." I went upstairs, and when I went upstairs I found her seated on the box at the end of the room. She was naked with the exception of her boots and stockings. I was so struck with what I saw that I exclaimed, "Good heavens, Mrs Neale, whatever are you doing?" to which she replied, "Come over here and sit down beside me; I am going to lay here tonight." I took a step or two into the middle of the room, and asked her to dress herself, saying, "What will the consequences be if Mr Neale comes in and sees you in the condition you are in?" She again said, "Come here and sit down," and again repeated, "I am going to stay here this night." She asked me a third time to go to her, and at this time, she was seated in an upright position at the ottoman, and I went and stood at the end of it and placed my left hand on her shoulder and again begged of her to dress herself. Just at the time I was making this remark to her, her husband came to the top of the steps with a clay pipe in his mouth, smoking. He said immediately on seeing us, "Now you b—s I have caught you," and commenced using a lot of bad language, calling me a villain, a coward, and a number of other names. I left the end of the ottoman when I saw him first, and walked across the floor to meet him. He then said, "I'll smash you," or "I'll kill you," or words to this effect, and seized a sweeping brush similar to the one produced, and attempted to strike with it. I warded off the blow and said, "Don't strike, Neale; don't do anything; I will explain matters in the morning," I then went downstairs and left the place. Whilst all this was going on, Mrs Neale continued to sit in the same position on the ottoman. Whilst I was in the room I believe her clothes were on two chairs and part of them on the floor. I did not observe that there was a window broken in the room. The furniture in the room was in order. I only once have been in the upstairs room before, and that is many months ago. It was by the invitation of Mr Neale, to look at the gas stove. There are two entrances to the shop, one at the front and one at the side. On Friday night the front entrance was closed, but the side entrance was open, and I left by that means. When I left Mrs Neale in the room at the back of the shop she was uninjured.'

Mr Neill (defence) then proceeded to question Black with a view to understanding his relationship with Esther Neale.

Mr Neill – What time was it when you made your hurried exit from the side door? – About half-past eight.
Was it not nine o'clock or after? – Certainly not.
Just recollect? – It was just turned half-past eight o'clock.
Did you know the proper closing time was seven o'clock? – No, I did not.
Have you ever taken her home from the shop before? – No, but I have met her accidentally, put her into the tram, and went home with her.
Was her husband at home? – No, but her sons were.
How long is that ago? – Four or five months.
Is that the only time you had been to the house? – The only time.
Have you ever waited an hour-and-a-half for Mr Neale before? – No. About twenty minutes is the longest before.
When the front door of the shop is closed is not the shop comparatively darkened? – Yes, comparatively.
And how long did you stay in that darkened shop waiting for the woman putting her hat on? – About seven or eight minutes; not more.

How long were you in the back bedroom? – Three or four minutes.

Then you did stay three or four minutes with the naked woman in a shop where there was no-one but you and her-self? – I did.

You must have been very busily engaged, because you did not hear the husband come? – I did not.

He had boots on? – I do not know what he had on.

How many steps are there to get out of the room? – About ten or twelve.

Stone steps and uncovered? – Yes.

And you never heard him until he addressed you? – No.

You did not stop to explain? – No.

You must have been in a hurry to get away? – I did not run.

Did he throw a brush at you? – He did.

You must have run away or it would not have missed you? – I walked calmly out of the place.

The brush missed you? – Yes, it went by the side of me.

Mr Atkinson then questioned Black – Did you not think it very strange that Mrs Neale should ask you to go upstairs? – Not at all; she might not have been able to find her bag or something, and required my assistance.

Did she say she had lost anything? – No.

You say she said 'I am going to lie here tonight.' Are you sure she said 'tonight'? – Yes.

Have you been on the premises since? – No.

Why did you not explain to the husband? – Because he was excited and under the influence of drink, and I knew there would be no reasoning with him.

How many times did he strike at you? – Only once.

Was the deceased not taking her boots and stockings off when her husband came? – I do not know.

She had no chemise on? – No.

And the stockings down? – I do not know.

When was the last time you were in the shop? – About a fortnight before.

You did not tell Mr Neale your business when he caught you in the room? – No, sir.

You saw Mrs Neale naked, Mr Black? – Yes, sir.

And there was plenty of light in the room? – Oh yes, plenty, sir.

Seeing that naked form, if there had been any bruises upon it would you have seen them? – Oh yes, sir, I should.

Did she make any complaint to you of any violence having been used? – No, sir, not at that time.

Richard Senior, clerk, Airedale Road, Bradford, was next called, and stated that he was acquainted with the husband of the deceased woman. On Friday last, he saw him at Blake's Restaurant about nine o'clock at night. Neale then bid him good night, left the place, and witness followed a couple of minutes later. He had been with Mr Neale from seven o'clock in the evening until nine o'clock. The latter was slightly intoxicated on leaving.

The inquiry was then adjourned until 10 a.m. on Tuesday morning.

Mr J. G. Hutchinson (the Borough Coroner) resumed the inquest at the Town Hall.

Thomas Cartwright, the manager of the White Lion Vaults, Kirkgate, was the first witness called. He said he was acquainted with Francis Wm. Neale, the husband of the deceased. He came to the vaults at 9.40 on Friday night, and entered by the back door. He was without hat, and appeared a little excited. He had a bruise on his forehead, and asked witness to lend him a hat. Cartwright asked him what he had been doing to lose his hat, and he replied, 'There has been a fight in Darley Street opposite my shop with two young men. I have been trying to part them and lost my hat in the scuffle.' Witness asked him what kind of men they were, to which Neale replied, 'They look like two respectable young men, but I don't know who they were. They have had to take one of them to the Infirmary.' He was supplied with two penny worth of rum and a cigar, and after he had been given a hat he went away, he left by the back door, and witness did not see him again that night.

Chief Constable Mr Withers commented that Neale appeared a little the worse for drink, but not bad. Witness saw him about three o'clock in the afternoon at the vaults the same day. The mark on Neale's forehead appeared to have been recently done.

John Cockcroft, the landlord of the Airedale Inn, Otley Road, said the deceased was his cousin, and was about thirty-nine years of age. He last saw her alive on Friday morning last at 11.30 in the room over the shop in Darley Street. Her husband was present. They were quarrelling, and scattered about the floor were pots, pans, dishes and a number of other articles, in an untidy state. She wished to clean these articles, but Mr Neale wished her to wash herself and go into the shop to business. Witness made the same request, but she refused to comply with it and answered 'I won't.' They were both in high temper, and he (Cockcroft) asked them to 'calm down' and left them. He next saw Mr Neale at 10.40 in the evening at the Airedale Inn.

Samuel Lodge, police surgeon, Wakefield Road, said, 'On 2 June about noon I made a post-mortem examination of the body of Esther Neale at the mortuary. Externally I found black marks at the left side of the back, which were not evident the night before. The body was that of a healthy well-developed woman. On opening the abdomen I found it full of fresh blood arising from the vessels about the left kidney. The kidney was healthy, but surrounded by clotted blood. I found five ribs fractured on the left side, some of them in two places. One of the fractured ribs had lacerated the vessels of the left kidney and penetrated inwardly to the cavity of the abdomen, then perforated, causing the cavity to become filled with blood. From the vessels of the kidneys into the abdomen there would be an escape of about 10lbs of blood. The stomach and intestines were removed and found quite healthy. The stomach contained undigested vegetable food. The liver, pancreas, kidneys, bladder were all healthy. On opening the chest the heart was found to be large and fat, but not soft, and there was no disease. The lungs were quite perfect, but the left side of the chest contained a large quantity of blood caused by a sharp point of the seventh rib which was fractured and bad penetrated the pleural cavity. Every rib below the chest was fractured. There was no external appearance of these terrible injuries on the Friday night, but they became evident on the Saturday. The bruise on the temple and near the orbit did not extend beneath the muscles. A large swelling on the body was carefully examined, and found the blood of recent origin. The brain was a fine one

William James Waugh, the barrister for William Francis Neale.

and healthy, but bloodless. Cause of death was fracture of the ribs, and consequent internal bleeding. After the injuries he would expect almost immediate death.

Police Constable Parsons was next called, and stated that on Friday night last about 10.55 he was on duty in Kirkgate, where he met the witness Cockcroft, whom he accompanied to a shop in Darley Street, where he found the body of a woman apparently dead. The body was stretched out on the floor and an overcoat had been placed over it.

There was also a chemise and red waist, and boots and stockings on the body, and the head was resting on a jacket. There was some blood on the floor near to the window, portions of a broken clay pipe, and a quantity of glass from a broken window. He looked for the deceased's clothing, but could not find any except what was on the body. He afterwards, however, found some clothing in the back yard. After he had been there ten minutes the husband came in, and Cockcroft asked him if he had got a doctor, and he replied, 'I have been to Dr Tacey's, and he could not come, and told me to go to Dr Taylor's, but I did not go.'

The husband made a statement in his presence, which PC Gibson wrote down at the time. Witness took Neale into custody and charged him on suspicion of having caused the death of his wife. The prisoner replied, 'I am not guilty.' Witness found the brush produced in the shop down-stairs, and he also produced the chemise, flannel vest, boots, a pair of stockings, and an overcoat found in the room.

'The husband made another statement to me in the corridor of the police cells on Sunday morning about a quarter past two, whilst I was in charge of him. He said, "This is a bad job; I wish I could see the end of it. There is nobody can say that I deliberately did it, because I did not. I did kick her, but that could not kill a woman in her state."'

This closed the evidence, and Mr Neill (defence), prior to the Coroner addressing the jury, drew his attention to the law on the subject of homicide, which said that homicide was not rendered justifiable or excusable by provocation, but if provocation was given to such an extent as to greatly excite the man who killed, manslaughter was the extent of the guilt. He also pointed out that if a man caught his wife in the act of adultery and killed someone on the spot, the guilt was manslaughter only.

The Coroner, addressing the jury, said after having had the opportunity of viewing the place in question and hearing the evidence in detail that he thought they would not have any very great difficulty in giving an opinion upon the case. Referring to the medical testimony, there could be no doubt as to the cause of death. It was due to the fracture of the ribs and subsequent internal bleeding, and on that point also the jury could have no difficulty. Then came the question of who caused these injuries and by whom were they inflicted.

The circumstances of the case were very distressing as detailed so far. The deceased had been a person who had given way to the drink, and she and her husband had quarrelled on trivial matters which ordinary people would not have done. Proceeding to refer to the evidence as given by the witnesses, and alluding to the time when the deceased was discovered in a nude state with the man Black, he remarked that they could well understand the condition in which the husband became, he finding his wife with a person whom he had regarded as a friend. No one would wonder at the language which was said to have been used by him, because he must have felt himself greatly insulted by the conduct of his wife and Black. Then came the question as to how and by whom those injuries had been caused. So far as Black was concerned, the jury would observe that Black went away and left the deceased seated upon an ottoman, and there was no evidence whatever to show that Black had returned, and under the circumstances, whether he had been guilty of gross immorality or not, it was very unlikely that he would return after what had taken place. It was not suggested either by the statement of the husband or any of the other witnesses that the woman was subjected to violence whilst Black was there, and there was nothing to show that she was.

The husband had confessed to having seen the chemise on his wife, and from its condition this must have been on the woman at the time she received the injuries. Neale was the only person present. He remained after having run Black out of the place. He admitted this, and after remaining there for some time went to a public house where he sought to borrow a hat. This went to show that the man had lost his hat, and he had to account for this. His explanation was that a quarrel had occurred outside his shop between two men, and that one of them had been taken to the infirmary. There had been no evidence to show that such was the case, and there was no truth in the story. Further, according to Black, when he was in the room, Mrs Neale's clothing was on two chairs and a portion on the floor, but on the place being visited by the police it was not there. Look out of the window, it is suggested, and there in the yard is the clothing together with a black hat. It was true no one had been able to identify it as the property of Mr Neale, but it was interesting to note that the one found and the one worn by Mr Neale were both black ones, and that on the Friday night he had to borrow one. The question then arose what was Neale doing with his wife? He says he found his wife in a fit, but the medical evidence negatived this statement, and showed that death was due to fractures

The cells located in the basement at Bradford Town Hall where William Francis Neale was kept.

and loss of blood. What, however, did Neale do, supposing his wife had been in a fit? He gave no alarm, although he subsequently visited the vaults and made the excuse about his hat, and after staying there a time he made his way to Otley Road. On arrival, there he was crying and trembling. The crying could be attributed to Neale acting on the impulse of the moment, and in a passion people, often cried and trembled when they realised their crime and consequences. Then again Neale did not bring a doctor when he might have done. When the police visited the place they found the body laid out as if for burial with the hands by the side, and when it was examined blood was found to have been wiped off by some person or other. Neale, on seeing his wife in this state, showed no signs of dismay, but gave some explanation to the officers present that those statements did not implicate anyone else or show that any other person had been on the premises after Black had left. Then there was also the statement to Constable Gibbons in the cells, where Neale said he did not do the deed deliberately. No one, said the Coroner, would suggest that the deed had been done in cold blood and with the intention to kill, but it was most extraordinary to find that the post-mortem examination revealed traces of a kick at the part of the body where the husband admitted having kicked his wife.

The jury must bear all those facts in mind, and after careful consideration say who had been guilty for this considerable violence. Alluding to the evidence of the witness Black he pointed out Black must have been longer in the room with the deceased than he had admitted. Whether he was there for immoral purposes or whether he was merely the victim of circumstances, it was clear, however, the woman had received no injury when he made his hurried departure on the appearance of the husband. There could be no question that the deceased had been guilty of the greatest indecency it was possible for any woman to be guilty of, but although she may have been guilty of indecency it did not justify violence being used to her such as to deprive her of her life. That would be absolutely no excuse and no justification for the husband killing her or using violence which would cause her death. They all knew homicides were murder, but there was a very important element in the law which said that a murder must be accompanied with malice and aforethought. The question for them to consider was if this violence was inflicted under provocation, which would bring it under the head of manslaughter, and by whom the violence was inflicted.

The jury then retired, and after an absence of five minutes returned into court with a verdict of manslaughter against the husband of the deceased woman.

Neale was then put before the Coroner, and committed for trial at the next Leeds Assizes.

THE TRIAL OF WILLIAM FRANCIS NEALE

At the Crown Court at the Leeds Assizes on 31 July 1888 before Mr Justice Smith – the trial of Francis William Neale, draper; of Darley Street, Bradford, for the manslaughter of his wife, Esther Neale, on June 1st, commenced. His Lordship took his seat promptly at ten o'clock, Mr B. Stansfeld and Mr Whittaker Thompson prosecuted. Mr Waugh (instructed by Messrs Neil and Broadbent) defended the prisoner Mr T. R. D., Wright (instructed by Mr J. Freeman) held a brief to watch the case on behalf of John Black, whose name has been prominently mixed up in the unhappy affair. Prisoner, as was the case before the inquest, seemed in a rather weak state of health. There was not a large attendance in court of the public, and ladies were not admitted.

Mr Stansfeld in opening the case said no doubt the jury had already read columns of the newspaper matter connected with the tragedy they were about to inquire into, but he asked them to put altogether out of their mind anything they might have read, and decide the case as against the prisoner purely and simply on the evidence placed before them. The prisoner and his wife had been married for some 19 years, and for the first portion of their married life they had lived happily together, but unfortunately from the intemperance of the deceased frequent quarrels had taken place between her and the prisoner at the bar. There was, however, another incident connected with the case, and that was of an immoral character.

There had undoubtedly been conduct of a very immoral character on the part of the Esther Neale, and during the six weeks of the life of the unfortunate woman the quarrels with the prisoner had been more frequent and for two or three days prior to her death he had rarely been in a state of sobriety. Such had been the violence of the quarrels that on two or three occasions a police officer from the free Library, attracted by the cries proceeding from the business premises of the prisoner, had gone there for the purpose of preventing any injury being inflicted on either part. Only on the 29th of May the same officer went there on hearing cries of 'Murder,' but though the prisoner had had time on that occasion to inflict injury, he had not done so. Despite all this, however, continued Mr Stansfeld, he was bound to inform the jury that no matter how great the provocation, it did not justify the prisoner on the charge he was placed in the dock for to-day. All this was connected with the case, but not really material. What the jury had to decide was to decide whether or not the prisoner at the bar had caused the death of his wife. Without further words

43

he would proceed to detail the facts of the case as occurred on 1st of June. On that day the deceased went to the shop about 11 o'clock, and even at such an early hour as that she was not perfectly sober.

His Lordship – Come to the proceedings of the evening about Black. I have read the interminable depositions, some of which have nothing to do with the case. We want to know what happened at the occurrence and afterwards.

Mr Stansfeld said he would accede to his Lordship's wishes. During the day of the deceased's death there were frequent quarrels between the prisoner and his wife. In the morning in one of the quarrels he knocked the deceased against a recess or cupboard in an upstairs room in the shop. That showed he was very angry with his wife and it had something to do with what happened afterwards.

At seven o'clock on the evening of 1 June, there were in the shop in Darley Street, Miss Bentley (the assistant), Mrs Neale, and her son Willie. At that time the prisoner they would hear it from the evidence of a man named Richard Seanor, was at Blake's Restaurant and remained there until about 8.40. After seven o'clock a man named John Black came into the shop, and ultimately Miss Bentley, and then the son, Willie, went away, and Mrs Neale and Black were left alone together except for customers who came in from about 7 o'clock to 8.50, at which time the prisoner returned. This was the part of the case which he (the learned counsel) said was grossly immoral. After Mrs Neale and Black had been in the shop some time, Mrs Neale went upstairs to an upper room, and having been there some little time Black was called up to the room. What state he found Mrs Neale in he (Black) would describe, but so far as he (Mr Stansfeld) could gather the evidence showed that the deceased had stripped herself of all her attire except her boots and stockings.

Black seemed to have noticed her state from outside the door of the room, and he Mr (Stansfeld) could not understand his subsequent conduct. One would have thought that seeing a woman in that position he would have retired, but Black did not appear to have done so. He appeared to have gone into the room, and he must have been in the room with the woman in that state for some period. Prisoner returned to the shop as stated about 8.50 p.m., and went into the room and saw his wife in the state of nudity, with the man Black standing near her, and one of his hands upon her shoulder. Speaking not as a lawyer, not as counsel for the Crown, but as a man to men, if he (the learned counsel) had been in the prisoner's position he should have acted as the prisoner had done; he should have seized the first weapon which came to hand and made straight for the man who he should think was defiling and seducing his wife. That was what the prisoner did. Having pursued Black without avail, if prisoner returned with the same frenzy on him and belaboured his wife and brought about her death, then he would be guilty of manslaughter. This is what the prosecution said he did. Counsel then proceeded to trace the movements of Neale during the evening. Prisoner told Cartwright that two young men had been fighting outside his shop in Darley Street, that they were respectable looking, and he attempted to separate them and lost his hat in the struggle.

Cartwright then gave prisoner a hat, and he went away. Cartwright had seen the prisoner between three and four in the afternoon and noticed his appearance, but did not notice that he had a slight bruise on his forehead. That was another incident which led the prosecution to say that it was between 9 and 9.40 that night the prisoner had been engaged in a scuffle, which resulted in the death of his wife.

44

Having got his hat the prisoner proceeded again to the shop in Darley Street. When he arrived there the better man asserted it-self in him again. He must have seen his wife in the terrible state in which she was, and he administered to her wants or tried to attend to her because they had in the evidence that the blood from the body had been wiped by a cloth. At 10.40 the prisoner presented himself at the house of John Cockcroft, innkeeper Otley Road, a cousin of the deceased, and said to him 'I believe Etty is dead.' Cockcroft said 'How do you know that?' and prisoner replied, 'I cannot rouse her.' After further conversation Cockcroft said 'Had you fetched a doctor?' and he said 'No,' where upon Cockcroft suggested that he should fetch one, and followed him to the shop. Prisoner appeared greatly excited and could scarcely speak. Cockcroft proceeded to the shop, and on his way met two policemen and with them went to the shop and found the body of the deceased lying a few feet away from the door. Counsel then proceeded to describe the injuries the deceased had received.

PLEADING GUILTY

Mr Waugh then rose, and said that after the exceedingly fair opening of his friend the counsel for the prosecution, he was prepared to advise his client to withdraw his plea of 'not guilty' and plead 'guilty.' He felt that if the case proceeded he could not make out what he supposed he would have to do, and make a perfect defence, namely that the violence was not unlawful. The Crown admitted the provocation was great, in fact they based the case upon the fact that the provocation was so great that it was almost impossible for any man to resist doing as he did the prisoner. What he did in making such a shocking discovery was done under excitement, and the great provocation he had received. No doubt a scuffle did take place and the violence used had caused the death of the unfortunate woman. Concluding, Mr Waugh called attention to the fact that already the prisoner had been in custody two months and in addition that prior to the occurrence his client had borne a good character and he was prepared to call witnesses who would speak to the inoffensive disposition of the prisoner.

His Lordship – You plead guilty then.
Mr Waugh – Yes.
His Lordship, addressing himself to the prison – You have pleaded guilty to a charge of manslaughter of your wife on the 1st of June, 1888?
Prisoner – Yes, my Lord.

His Lordship, continuing, said there were circumstances in the case which made him feel for prisoner and for the position in which he stood. Neale had a wife undoubtedly of drunken habits, from the deposition it appeared he had reason to suspect she was carrying on the life of adulteress until June 1st. On that evening he went home and found his wife in a state of nudity with a man named Black. He then did that what as the learned counsel for the prosecution rightly said any man of feeling would have kicked Black downstairs, and hurried him into the streets, but after that returned to the house in a paroxysm of rage prisoner turned upon his wife and the consequence was he now stood in the dock on a charge of manslaughter. But there were manslaughters and there were manslaughters. Already the prisoner had been months in jail, and his Lordship said he couldn't bring himself to pass any further sentence upon than one day's imprisonment, which would mean he would be discharged.

William Francis Neale then left the dock a free man because in some eyes it was felt he was perfectly justified in his murderous attack on his wife.

There was an attempt at applause in court, which was quickly suppressed.

After his acquittal, Neale was remarried in September 1893 to a Miss Mary Alice Allison at Bolton, St James. The short marriage ended in 1897 when Mary died, aged just thirty-five. There is no record of a suspicious death for Mary, so we must presume she died by means other than her husband's boot. Francis lived on until April 1905, when he died in Bradford, aged fifty-eight.

Leeds Town Hall, where the Assizes were held.

James Kirkby
Double Murder and Suicide, 1888

TERRIBLE TRAGEDY AT MANNINGHAM
Double Murder and Suicide

A tragedy of a terrible character was brought to light on Sunday evening at Manningham, the dead bodies of a murdered wife and child and their supposed murderer being discovered in a house in Church Street, where during the day congregations had been peacefully worshipping. The house in which the ghastly discovery was made at No. 35, Church Street, and the family amongst who the terrible tragedy was committed was of the name of Kirkby. The family consisted of James Kirkby, aged 27 years, Alice Kirkby, his wife aged 25 years, Beatrice their eldest daughter, aged 3 years, and an infant son named Tom, aged 11 months.

Illustrated Weekly Telegraph
Saturday 24 November 1888

The Murder

In November 1888, the country as a whole was very much preoccupied with the murderous reign of terror perpetrated by the now infamous Jack the Ripper. Every day, the population scoured the newspapers for snippets of information relating to the intensive investigation being carried out into the serial murders, that had taken place in the district of Whitechapel, East London. The final accredited ripper murder – that of Marie Jeanette Kelly – had occurred only as recently as 9 November, just days before James Arthur Kirkby consigned his wife and young son to an early grave. We will never know what motive inspired James to destroy his family, even if it was Jack the Ripper himself, because he left no written explanation and took his terrible secret to the tomb. If only his immediate neighbour, Ellen Bowden, had intervened upon hearing the bedroom window crashing to the ground and the sound of repeated screams to be let up on the morning of 18 November, then the lives of Alice, her unborn child and infant son might well have been spared. It was indeed a tragedy in itself that Ellen, who lived at No. 37, simply went back into her house, where a short time later she heard the sound of footsteps going down the stairs in No. 35 before silence descended. Throughout the rest of the day, the blinds in the windows of No. 35 remained down and the house closed; not one member of the family was seen about the neighbourhood. Remarkably, even this did not induce any suspicion in the neighbours that something might be amiss.

It was not until around 10 p.m. later that day, when the sound of a small child continually crying from within the house was heard, that action was finally taken. Word was sent to Alice's widowed mother, Elizabeth Waite, who lived close by at Oak Lane, that there may be a problem. Mrs Waite, who had not seen her daughter since the previous Thursday, at once made her way to her daughter's house, where she found the house in darkness with both the front and back doors securely locked, as well as the windows. In a state of distress after hearing three-year-old Beatrice crying from inside, Mrs Waite went straight to Manningham police station, where she reported her concerns to Sub-Inspector Bentley. The sub-inspector, sensing the urgency of the situation, went at once to the Kirkby residence, taking Police Constables Hardisty and Phillips along with him, and upon reaching the destination instructed them to go round the back and force their way in.

Police Constable Hardisty was the first in – wasting no time, he smashed the scullery window to gain access. As the constable navigated his way through the dark house, he started to climb the open staircase. What he saw in the darkness was to fill him with horror, for at the top of the stairs, suspended by a piece of rope attached to a hook in the ceiling, was the body of James Kirkby. Just as the constable was

Alice Kirkby, following her death.

PC Hardisty discovers the body of James Kirkby.

regaining his composure, he found Alice Kirkby laid face down on the floor near the front bedroom door, her head facing the bed. Alice, who was in the later stages of pregnancy, was naked but for her nightdress and had a rope wrapped tightly three times around her neck. The constable removed the rope, even though it was evident from her blackened facial features and protruding tongue that she was quite dead. Moving over to the bed, he tentatively peeled back the bedclothes, where he was shocked to discover the lifeless body of a baby, Tom. Just like his mother, he had a rope around his neck and had been strangled in a similar way. Looking around, it was apparent to the constable from the general disorder in the bedroom that a great struggle had occurred. Making his way back down the stairs, he found little Beatrice, with whom he was already acquainted. She was sitting on the floor of the kitchen crying. Gently taking hold of the frightened but uninjured child, who was undressed, he asked her softly, 'Beatrice, what are you doing here?' to which she replied, 'Mamma is in bed.'

After PC Hardisty had unlocked the door and handed Beatrice to a neighbour, he and the other officers cut down the body of James Kirkby. Within minutes, James Withers, the Chief Constable, was informed of the tragedy at his home in St Pauls Road, a short distance away. The Chief Constable instructed Sub-Inspector Bentley to fetch Mr Mossop, a surgeon, which he accordingly did. However, he could do no more than state that death in all three cases had occurred several hours previously.

Manningham police station at Bavaria Place, where Elizabeth Waite reported her suspicions that all was not well at her daughter's home.

Lister's Mill, where James Kirkby was employed as an engine tender.

Mr Withers, on viewing the scene, was not in the slightest doubt that Alice and her son had been deliberately murdered by husband and father James Kirkby who, after having killed them, hanged himself. The Chief Constable taking charge of the crime scene made all the arrangements he could before leaving the house in the charge of Sub-Inspector Bentley for the night.

James and Alice Kirkby had been married for about four years prior to the tragedy. He was in full-time work at Lister's Mills close by and was employed as an engine tender. The family appeared to have a good standard of living. The house the family shared was an old-fashioned cottage raised above the level of the road, with a pretty rockery at the front overlooking the corner of St Paul's church. The cottage was furnished very comfortably for a man of his means, despite the family sharing one bed in the front room, which overlooked Church Street. According to the statements made by the neighbours to reporters, the couple had occasional quarrels but nothing that would ever indicate that the husband was capable of murder. Kirkby himself, though sometimes fond of a drink, was not thought of as a bad character, and his wife was regarded by people locally as industrious and a good mother and wife. It was revealed by some, however, that James had a jealous streak, although there was, as far as anyone knew, not the slightest justification for this.

The site of No. 35 Church Street.

The Investigation

As investigations by the police progressed over the following days, it appeared that around eight o'clock on the morning of the murders, Kirkby had got out of bed and dressed himself in readiness. When his body was found hanging, he was dressed in trousers and a sleeve vest as though he had been going about the house. All the evidence inclined the police to believe that the murders were pre-meditated. When Kirkby had got up that morning, he had taken great care to not wake his wife, and while she was lying asleep he had put one of three pieces of washing line he had cut earlier around her neck. The state of the bedroom indicated that Alice, who was a strong woman, had fought back bravely, which was witnessed by the neighbour who had heard the window breaking and Alice demanding to be let go. The evidence further suggested she had either been dragged out of bed by the end of the rope, or struggled and fallen to the floor as she attempted to remove the rope around her neck and save herself. The question that will never be answered, and baffled the investigators and locals alike, was why James Kirkby chose to kill his small son, and spare his young daughter's life. It may have been that Beatrice, witnessing the attack on her mother, managed to hide herself away before the third piece of washing line could be put around her neck and that her father, realising the enormity of his crime, used it to kill himself instead.

On Monday 19 November, the Borough Coroner (Mr J. G. Hutchinson) opened the inquest at the town hall into the circumstances resulting in the death of Alice Kirkby, aged twenty-five years; James Arthur Kirkby, her husband; and Tom Kirkby, aged eleven months, their infant son; all of whom were discovered dead at their residence. Supt. Campbell was present on behalf of the police. First to be sworn in was Elizabeth Waite, of Oak Lane, Manningham, who deposed that the deceased, Alice Kirkby, was her daughter, and was the wife of James Arthur Kirkby, a machine tender, employed at Manningham Mills. Elizabeth had last seen her alive on Thursday night last at No. 35 Church Street, in the company of her husband. The deceased did not make any complaint that night, but in her husband's presence she had previously complained of his ill treatment. About three months ago, on a Saturday night, Elizabeth called at her daughter's house. On that occasion, James Kirkby had called her either a 'pig' or a 'liar'. Her daughter complained that night about him abusing her every Saturday night, and that 'she did not like to go home at night'. Elizabeth asked him why he went on in that way, but he replied, 'Oh, nothing; she should not talk so much.'

Elizabeth then 'told him a little of her mind,' but he only answered, 'I wish you would say what you have to say and have done with it.' Her daughter had never complained to her about any violence on the part of her husband, but she had said that he 'had done worse'. Elizabeth had since heard, however, that he had tied her down in bed. It had been her daughter's practice to visit her house every Saturday or Sunday, and as she did not come on Sunday, the witness went to her house around six o'clock, thinking that something was the matter. On arriving there, she found the house locked up and, on looking through the window, she saw that the fire was out and that the clothes horse was standing in the middle of the floor. She thought they must have gone out to pay a visit, and went away. During the evening, two other persons with whom Mrs Kirkby worked called upon her and asked about her daughter, but it was not until around ten o'clock that she heard anything that seemed suspicious. Her daughter's husband was not a very sober man, but she did not know that he was violent. He came from some place wide of York.

The coroner then examined the evidence of Sub-Police Constable Hardisty before swearing in Sub-Inspector Bentley. He stated that there was a piece of rope round the neck of the child found in the bed. The rope was drawn very tight. He had examined all the ropes that had been used, and was of the opinion they had all originally formed one piece. On searching the house, he did not find any suicide letters. At this stage, the inquiry was then adjourned until Wednesday, when, after examining Ellen Boden's evidence, the coroner called Dr Mossop of Manningham. The doctor gave evidence to the effect that on Sunday evening, at around five past ten, he saw the dead body of Alice Kirkby, at which time the body was lying on the floor in the bedroom, and the cord had been removed from the neck. He examined it, and found that the body was that of a well-built and well-nourished female. The surface of the body was pale, with the exception of the face and upper portion of the neck. The tongue protruded from the mouth, and was livid and swollen. There were three abrasions on the neck to the right of the windpipe, each about the size of a sixpence. The neck was also indented as if by pressure from a cord. She was pregnant, in his opinion being some seven months advanced.

The coroner then asked, 'Have you formed any opinion as to about how long the woman had been dead?'

Dr Mossop replied 'The body was perfectly cold, and I think that in all probability death had taken place at least ten hours before I saw her. The cause of death was due to strangulation caused by direct pressure on the windpipe by a cord.'

Responding, the coroner said, 'It had been stated that the cord was tied three times round the neck. I suppose it would be impossible for a person to tie the rope so many times tight by oneself?'

The Doctor replied in the affirmative. This concluded the evidence, and the coroner proceeded to address the jury. There could be, said he, little doubt as to the cause of death. They would recollect that it was stated a cord was found tied three times round the deceased's neck, and so tight that it would have been impossible for the deceased woman to do it herself. That therefore did away with the theory of suicide on the part of the woman. The evidence showed that there was nobody in the house who could have done it except the children, and they were so young that it would be impossible to suppose that anyone but the husband had inflicted the injuries. If they believed that was the case, the jury would have to return a verdict that the woman had been murdered by her husband.

After a few minutes in consultation, the jury returned a verdict of 'wilful murder' against the husband, James Arthur Kirkby. The coroner then proceeded to review the evidence with regard to the death of the infant, Tom. He said that he was found dead in the house at the same time as his mother on Sunday night last, and there could be no doubt that the cause of the death for the child was strangulation.

Then came the question of who inflicted the injuries. There was no one in the house who could have caused them except the father or mother, and if they believed the evidence and took into consideration the verdict returned in the last case, they must come to the conclusion that the boy had been murdered by his father. In this case, the jury also returned a verdict of 'wilful murder' against the father himself. Mr Hutchinson, referring to the death of the man James Arthur Kirkby, the husband of Alice and father of the boy Tom, said the jury would have to inquire by what means he had come to his death. At the same time as the other two, he was discovered dead in the house at Church Street, suspended by the neck with a cord attached to a hook at the top of the stairs. There could be little doubt that the immediate cause of death in this case was strangulation.

As the jury were satisfied that the man had hung himself, they then had to consider the state of his mind. The coroner said he must impress upon the jury that the law considered all persons as sane and responsible for their acts until sufficient evidence was presented to prove the contrary. In this case, the evidence went to show that the man's mind was not affected. He apparently indulged in bad language, but that was not sufficient to justify the conclusion that his mind was affected. They would have to consider the context of the case. The coroner then went on to review the evidence specifically concerning the actions of the husband, and pointed out that the condition in which the woman was found demonstrated that the man must have been most determined in his intention. The breaking of the window also reflected this. He tied the rope once, tied it again, and then a third time, so tightly on all three occasions that only one such knot would have been sufficient to extinguish a life. This, along with the other facts, went to show that the man knew what he was doing, and had a firm intention. There was no evidence, save the mad act itself, to show that the man's mind was at all affected. If committing such an act, however, were sufficient to render people liable to be considered in a state of temporary insanity, life would never be taken by any sane person. It was entirely for the jury to decide the condition of the man's mind, but in the absence of any evidence showing that Kirkby's mind was temporarily affected, the proper verdict to return would be of *felo de se*.

The jury retired, and as they were doing so the coroner said, 'You will bear in mind there is no evidence before you that the man's mind has been affected before, or anything of the kind.'

The jury, after being absent for about three quarters of an hour, did indeed deliver this verdict. *Felo de se* was a somewhat antiquated verdict even back in 1888, having long been superseded for the more modern one of 'temporary insanity'. The Bradford coroner James Hutchinson was convinced there was no hope for Kirkby, and took care to convey his opinion to the jury in plain speaking, with the result that they found the murderer to be fully in control of his actions. As a result, James Kirkby was deprived of a Christian burial service administered by the clergy, although it is believed that a friend read a sermon at his funeral instead.

St Paul's church, Manningham.

James Harrison
Wife Murder, 1890

HORRIBLE MURDER IN BRADFORD

One of the most brutal and cruellest murders that has ever stained the records of Bradford was perpetrated early this morning at 7, Lord Street, a little side street of cottages off Wakefield Road, on the left-hand side, just above the railway bridge, and about a mile from the Town Hall. The victim is a married woman named Hannah Harrison, and the murderer her husband, James Harrison, a man 36 years of age, of notorious character, and with an unfavourable character record on the pay books at the Town Hall. The tragedy was committed shortly after 5 o'clock this morning and but for the previous life of the husband it would be altogether inexplicable. His ill treatment of the murdered woman, and his threats to go for her, have however, been common talk amongst the neighbours for some time past, and whilst sorrow for the victim and detestation of the crime is universal amongst them, surprise is entirely absent.

Bradford Daily Telegraph
12 May 1890

The Murder

When James Harrison told his aged foster mother, Bella Duckworth, that he was 'going to do it this morning', the old girl did not think for one minute he was on the verge of brutally murdering his wife. In fact, she thought it was a load of nonsense, and even when he went downstairs to get a carving knife, which he then attempted to hide, she still considered it to be a bluff. It was therefore with horror that, just seconds later, she watched him launch his attack on Hannah Harrison, who was known as Anne. Bella, frightened out of her wits, shouted at the couple's children to open the window and scream murder. A moment later, Bella herself, fearing for her own safety, ran into the street, clad only in her chemise and without any shoes, to raise the alarm. Meanwhile, James was busy carrying out his deadly threat. Having seized Anne by the hair, he did his best to stab her, but she fought back bravely, and even managed to get the knife out of his hands before begging for her life. 'Spare me,' she cried out loud. 'Spare me; if you don't like to go to that job stay at home! If you don't like to go, James, I will work and keep you while you get a night job!' Her plea for mercy was in vain, for the powerfully built Harrison then proceeded to drag the poor woman across the bedroom floor and down the stairs into the family room. Once there, he seized the poker from the fireplace and set about beating his wife about the head with the heavy instrument until her head was battered and her life was ended.

The couple's three children – Matilda, aged thirteen years, Alice Ann, aged eleven years, and Sophia, aged just ten – witnessed most of the attack, and ran out into the street in alarm while still in their nightclothes as the final scene of the tragedy took place. Fortunately for Anne, medical evidence later stated that so ferocious was the attack, she would have barely been conscious after the first initial blows. Despite the cries of 'murder' made by Bella Duckworth and the children, along with the thumping noises coming from the house, the neighbours were extremely reluctant to get involved because, according to one neighbour, Harrison was 'always ready with a bat for anyone', and his treatment of his wife was notorious in the area. In fact, it would be some thirty minutes after the murderous frenzy had commenced that a neighbour finally entered the house where he discovered the lifeless body of Anne at the foot of the stairs, and close by in the kitchen, the blood-stained poker and carving knife used to great effect during the cowardly murder. Looking around the living room, the neighbour noted that although there was little evidence to show that a struggle had taken place, the walls, table and chairs were splattered with blood. Possibly concerned that he might next be the focus of Harrison's uncontrollable rage, the neighbour fell short of investigating the one upstairs room the family shared, as James Harrison had lodged himself there.

Anne and James Harrison.

The first police officer to arrive on the scene was Acting Sergeant Foster from Bowling police station, who was in close proximity on Wakefield Road. Quite bizarrely, he found James Harrison smiling from his bedroom window at the large crowd that had gathered outside the house. The newly ordained murderer continued in his strange behaviour as Sergeant Foster escorted both him and the murder weapons to the police station. To onlookers, he appeared to be blissfully unaware of the enormity of his actions. Although he was walking in the shadow of the hangman's noose, he laughed and greeted people he knew with a cheery 'good morning' while en route, almost as though he was on a casual walk in the park. After taking him into custody at the police station, Foster cautioned him for causing the death of his wife, to which he replied, 'We had a few words: I cannot help it.' Later that day, Harrison was moved to the much larger police station within the town hall. Chief Constable James Withers and the police surgeon, Samuel Lodge, arrived at Lord Street at 8 a.m. to examine the murder scene where, frustratingly, they found the victim had already been laid out on the kitchen table by her concerned but misguided neighbours. Although forensics were very much a science of the future in 1890, the neighbours, thinking they were doing the dead woman a kindness by hastily cleaning up her injuries and wiping away the blood around her face, severely hampered the police surgeon's examination. The examination was further frustrated by the sheer volume of spectators wandering in and out of the heavily contaminated crime scene. Dr Lodge wasted no time in having the body removed to the mortuary by horse ambulance for a post-mortem. The police then locked up the house and took possession of the key.

At the time of the crime, Lord Street was made up of two rows of cottages. No. 7, where the Harrisons lived, was the middle house on the side nearest the centre of the town. The only difference between this and other back-to-back type houses in Bradford was the lack of a passageway leading to the houses at the rear. The living accommodation was made up of a good-sized room on the ground floor with a joint kitchen and sitting room, and one double bedroom above. Access to the bedroom was via a staircase running back across the house. The doorway leading to the staircase and the spot where Harrison dragged Annie to finish off the murder is shown in the sketch of the interior (p. 60). The drawing of the Harrisons (p. 58) was from a photograph taken not long after their marriage in 1878, and was regarded by the police to be a good likeness even twelve years later. Lord Street in 2013 is a collection of industrial units, the cottages demolished long ago.

The couple were well known in the Bowling area of Bradford where they lived. James Harrison, or 'Hock Harrison' as he was known, was considered by people locally to be a violent, lazy, drunken, quarrelsome and dangerous character, and not shy of raising his hand to his wife. Such was his reputation that no one dared to ever interfere with him or his domestic quarrels. At thirty-six years old, he had lived at Lord Street since he was just a fortnight old, and was the adopted son of Bella Duckworth, who was approaching eighty-one. On the day of the murder, Harrison was supposedly going back to work at the Messrs Ripleys' dyeworks for the first time in six weeks, where he had been employed off and on for the past twenty-five years as a dyer. More recently,

A contemporary sketch of the interior of No. 7 Lord Street.

A sketch of the exterior.

he had been sacked for bad timekeeping and being drunk on the job. During the time he was laid off, he had spent the majority of it drinking to excess while living off the meagre wages generated by Annie and his three children. Bella Duckworth made it known that in the days leading up to the murder, family life had been especially difficult. There had been an ongoing situation started during dinner about a piece of meat that had been sent by a relative for Sunday dinner, and James Harrison had taken issue. An argument had quickly developed between the couple when Harrison had said to his wife 'if you ever touch that meat I hope it will rot in your belly', and also further added that if she used the gravy it would scald her. As a result of the altercation, Mrs Harrison did not eat any of the meat and relations between the couple remained strained right up until he attacked his wife. It was thought by the neighbourhood that the motive for the murder was purely down to his anger and reluctance to give up his lazy lifestyle, but Bella was sure it was due to the recent problems over the joint of meat. There were conflicting accounts of Harrison that described him as being a very good husband and father when he was sober, one who cooked and cleaned and, when in work, delivered the last penny of his wages to his wife, but when drunk his temper was deemed to be uncontrollable. His brother had been also very fond of drink, and did little or no work. He was eventually admitted to the pauper lunatic asylum at nearby Menston, where he died not long after.

Hannah Harrison had, even by 1890 standards, led a pitiful existence. She was originally from Wakefield, but had lived in Bradford since she was sixteen. During her thirteen-year marriage to Harrison she had borne him eight children, but as child mortality was commonplace in those days, only three survived birth. For twelve of those thirteen years she had walked, pregnant or not, in all weather 2 miles every day to her job as a weaver at Holme Mills to help with the family's tight budget.

As news spread of the murder, reporters arrived at Lord Street seeking out background information on the family, and the neighbours wasted little time in describing the treatment doled out by the murderer to his downtrodden victim. 'He used to take on with her shamefully,' said one, which brought forth a multitude of stories relating to his brutality from the crowds that had gathered around. Another neighbour went on to say 'she was as decent a woman as ever walked, as good a wife as was ever tied to a man, but he was drunken, idle scum. He has been a prizefighter and a boxer, and was a hard-hearted one'. Thick and fast the crowd offered their thoughts, and someone else said, 'She never quarrelled with him, she just used to run out into the street when he was in a temper.' Another onlooker explained how all three of her children were half-timers at Swithin Anderton & Sons Eastbrook Mills. Sophia, the youngest, had only gone to the mill three weeks previously and had just drawn her first week's wage – 1s – the previous Saturday. This was a blessing to her mother, as she had remarked to a neighbour 'I shall be a bit better off now,' before proudly relating how the second oldest, Alice, had contributed 2s to get her little sister a new dress so she might go out dressed decently. 'They are three grand little lasses' were the closing words that fell upon the reporter's ears as he left the scene. 'It is a pity for them this has happened, their mother is better off. She is in a better place now, than she was on earth.' As is too often the case with a man of Harrison's character, he had a wife who was in every respect far too good for him.

The Investigation

The very same day, as news of the tragedy spread rapidly through the town, Harrison was brought before the magistrates' court and charged with murder. Although only a few hours had passed since the crime, a large crowd had already gathered outside the police court at the town hall long before eleven o'clock, when the magistrates sat. When the doors opened, the court was very quickly filled with eager spectators, who were generally ill informed as to the exact details of the murder. Shortly before the magistrates took their seats on the bench, the prisoner was observed in the dock. In the words of the court reporter, he was described as 'a rather tall man and of slight build. His hair is closely cropped and he wears a heavy moustache. Around his neck tied in a knot was a real handkerchief with white spots. Generally he had an unkempt and untidy appearance.' The reporter said 'he seemed entirely unconcerned, and spent the time before being called on in looking listlessly around the court'. The magistrates on the bench were Mr Skidmore, Mrs Stipendiary, Alderman Smith Feather, the former mayor, Alderman Moulson and Mr Arthur Briggs.

Mr Withers, the chief constable, rose at once and disappointed the court spectators, who thought there would be a lengthy account of the crime, by asking for a week-long remand for further enquiries. He said the prisoner, James Harrison, was charged with the murder of his wife, Hannah Harrison, between 5 and 5.30 that morning. He said he did not propose to go into the matter further than to call the officer who was summoned to the house and let him say what the prisoner stated when charged. Acting Sergeant Henry Foster told the court he was on duty at Bowling police station at 5.25 that morning when he heard a scream and went out on the road. He saw a crowd of people at the end of Lord Street, and on going to the street found the prisoner's three children in their nightdresses. He asked them what was the matter and they said their father had killed their mother. He then went into the prisoner's house in Lord Street and found the body of a woman in a pool of blood. He lifted her head up and saw it was a very serious case. He concluded that it was necessary to have a doctor, but as he could not get anyone to go for one, he asked a man to watch the door and went himself to Dr Butler's, about 140 yards away. Dr Butler came and pronounced life extinct. He took the prisoner into custody and cautioned him for causing the death of his wife. The sergeant said Harrison then told him, 'We had a few words: I cannot help it.' The verdict: was he sober? Perfectly.

The prisoner was remanded for a week.

On the afternoon of 12 May, the funeral of Hannah Harrison took place at Bowling Cemetery. Prior to the cortège leaving Lord Street, the coffin remained open at the family home in order that friends and neighbours could have a last look at the body.

Bowling police station.

So large was the crowd of people waiting to see Hannah that many had to be turned away. Those that were admitted were pleased to see that her face bore a perfectly natural expression, and very few marks that would indicate the violent nature of her death. The funeral left the house for the cemetery about 2.30 p.m., but for a short time before two o'clock, Lord Street, which was open at one end, was crowded with people, who despite the heavy rain remained patiently waiting. As it got closer to the time for the funeral procession to head to the cemetery at the clouds cleared and the sun began to shine. This change in weather brought many more people out to observe the procession, and by 2.30 p.m. Wakefield Road was extremely crowded. As the spectators waited, conversation naturally turned to the crime itself, and in particular the perpetrator. Nobody seemed to have a good word of any sort for James Harrison. 'He never was any good' appeared be the unanimously agreed upon verdict, and a hanging, according to the popular judgement, seemed 'too good for him'. 'But,' added one, 'if they don't hang him they be owt to hang them, cause he was no lunatic, she was far too good for him, and a few would have put up with as much as she had.' Soon after two o'clock, Sub-Inspector Barraclough, accompanied by six policemen, arrived on the scene and successfully cleared Lord Street. A few minutes before the cortège set off, the coffin containing the body of Mrs Harrison was carried down the street and placed on the hearse that stood in Wakefield Road. At the cemetery, the funeral service having been read, the body was then committed to the grave. The plate on the black coffin bore the inscription 'Anne Harrison, died 12th May, 1890, aged 38 years'.

Accordingly, as was the process, James Harrison was committed by the magistrates' court on a charge of murder and sent to the Summer Assizes at Leeds. When he was put before Mr Justice Charles, he maintained a carefree attitude. Either Harrison knew he was doomed or just simply did not care, either way, from the start of his

Bowling Cemetery, where Anne Harrison is buried.

trial he paid little or no attention to what was taking place, other than pleading not guilty to murder. Mr Mellor, the defending barrister, addressed the jury on his behalf, claiming his client had committed the offence through extreme provocation, but this was futile as there was very little sympathy for the hapless prisoner, who attributed his vile actions to a squabble over a joint of meat. In due course, the jury found him guilty, but they did recommend mercy. When the judge pronounced the sentence of death, he warned Harrison not to place too much hope on a reprieve. Despite the enormity of the ultimate penalty awarded against him, the prisoner simply stared at the jury before calmly turning and walking out of the dock in the direction of the cells. He appeared to court spectators to not have a single care in the world.

Following the verdict and sentence, a petition to reprieve Harrison was circulated in the Bowling district, but the signatures gathered were not sufficient to justify sending it forward to the Home Secretary. Mr J. J. Wright, who conducted his case when he was first arrested and before the magistrates, wrote to the Home Secretary, calling attention to the recommendation of mercy by the jury. He received the reply that the Home Secretary could not see a reason to adopt the recommendation.

While awaiting execution at Armley Prison, Harrison was constantly monitored by two prison officers, who attempted to ease his mind during the short time he had left on earth by reading books to him from the prison library. As was the usual privilege with capital sentences, he was also allowed to order nearly any type of food he wanted. Mutton chops, ham and eggs, beefsteaks and roast meat were supplied to him and despite his impending sentence, he truly relished his meals. During the last few days of his life, he started to pay deeper attention to the prison chaplain, and as no communication of any chance of a reprieve was received, he gradually came to the conclusion that he would have to suffer death at the hangman's hands, and prepared himself for his fate. One little relaxation of the rules permissible under the death sentence was the granting by the governor of a pipe and tobacco to the condemned man. During his last few days, he smoked no fewer than fourteen to sixteen ounces of thick twist.

On Saturday 23 August, Harrison had his last visits from those who were nearest to him. They took place during the afternoon, and were naturally distressing. The first people who visited him were two female cousins, who both urged Harrison to prepare for death, and he seemed to take notice of their request. With them, however, he was not particularly free in his conversation, but he was more communicative to some other friends, who brought with them Harrison's three young daughters. The surroundings of the visiting cell are not pleasant at any time. Harrison had to stand behind a massive row of iron bars while his visitors stood some 3 or 4 feet away, with the warders seated between them. To his later visitors, Harrison repeatedly complained that he had been provoked by his wife, but said he was truly sorry for what he had done and hoped for forgiveness. In tears, he told his friends he was now fully prepared to die, and only hoped for a late reprieve for the sake of his young children. In the one and only farewell letter James Harrison was to send from his condemned cell, he bid an affectionate farewell to his children. The letter was

Armley Gaol, where James Harrison paid the full price for his ghastly murder.

written late on the night before his execution by a warder, at his dictation. In the letter he requested that the children be happy, and nice to people they meet in life, and expressed the hope that they would all meet again in heaven.

THE WIFE MURDER AT BOWLING
Execution of Harrison

On Tuesday the 26th of August, sharp at the stroke of eight o'clock, the black flag was hoisted again over the summit of Armley prison, to denote the execution of James Harrison, for the murder of his wife at Bowling. There were not many spectators around the prison walls, fewer indeed than usually gratify their curiosity by catching a glimpse of the floating black flag. The workmen as they passed to and fro cast a glance at the awe-inspiring black walls and then passed on. The women folk lingered a while and discussed the merits of the case, and they too passed quickly aside. There was no manifest outward interest in the fate of the man. As the hour for the execution rapidly approached, there were a few score who hung about the roadside and in the fields below waiting out of idle curiosity to see the black flag hoisted, as in passing and out of equal curiosity they had seen others before when greater criminals than James Harrison had suffered their last doom in Armley Prison. Billington, the hangman, who has the engagements at Armley, arrived there on Monday afternoon, and was located in the prison, and in consequence of recent instructions from the Home Office and the introduction of a new governor, information is somewhat difficult to obtain. Under such circumstances, it is difficult to state the details which occurred, but it is stated that the drop was six feet two. Before this, it was hoped there would have been a new 'execution chamber' on very much improved principles. It has not yet come into being, and it may be hoped it will not be required. The hangman's chamber is at present in the old 'wheelhouses', where criminals used to tread the wheel and within which Otto Brand, Johnson, well known in Bradford, West, and other murderers have met their just doom. The last execution which took place here was on New Year's Day of this year, and on the last day of 1889 there was a double execution. Major Lane, the governor of the prison, read to Harrison on Sunday the decision of the home secretary, which we published yesterday, and with that his last ray of hope vanished. The culprit received it calmly and collectively as far as outward indications would show, but there was never the less indication that he had hoped that the last dread penalty of the law would not be enforced. His daughters, by special permission, again paid him a visit yesterday afternoon, and the parting and grief it is not well to dwell upon. Harrison, after seeing his daughters yesterday afternoon, was visited by the chaplain of the prison, the Rev Mr Bower, and in the evening became somewhat calmer. He partook of a light supper and retired to rest at 11.45 p.m. On retiring to rest, the condemned man asked that he should be awakened early, but there was no need for the request, as he himself was aroused by a slight knocking in the neighbourhood of the cell at 5.45. He dressed himself, and doing so quietly observed that he supposed that it was now too late to hope for a reprieve. This was the only observation he made to the warders. The chaplain paid him an early visit, and remained with him in prayer in the condemned cell. The wretched man in the last few hours exhibited more traces of inward consciousness and emotion than he had previously done.

The preparations for the execution were begun shortly before eight, when James Billington proceeded to the cell and adjusted some of the straps. The bell from the chapel was tolling, thus announcing the approach of the final moment for the little procession of prison officials, the Under Sheriff and warders from the cell to the scaffold, the chaplain on the way repeating the words of the funeral service. At the lead of the procession walked the governor, Major Lane, and the Under Sheriff (Mr Edwyn Gray, of York). Then came the chaplain, followed by the executioner, and the culprit between two warders, with Chief Warden Taylor in charge of the posse of warders bringing up the rear. With a firm step, Harrison walked unassisted to the scaffold, casting at times a furtive glance heavenwards. He never opened his lips on the way to the scaffold; when on it did not respond to the prayers of the chaplain, and died without a passing reference to his awful crime or the dreadful surroundings amid which he met his death. The pause on the scaffold was of the most momentary character, and the six feet two inches drop which Billington gave the condemned man caused instantaneous death, with less than the usual amount of muscular twitching observable on such occasions. To those outside, the floating of the black flag in a strong breeze and a brief glimpse of sunshine gave the customary indication that the law of the land had once more been vindicated.

The Illustrated Weekly Telegraph
Saturday 30 August 1890

An explanation for the great firmness exhibited by Harrison at his execution may be found in the question put to him three days previously by a relative: 'Do you think you'll duff?' 'Nay,' replied Harrison, 'I shan't duff if I were to be hanged twice over.'

Thomas Bentley
Murder and Suicide, 1894

TERRIBLE TRAGEDY IN BRADFORD
A WOMAN MURDERED BY HER HUSBAND
BEATEN TO DEATH WITH A HAMMER
SUICIDE OF THE MURDERER

This forenoon, a terrible tragedy was enacted in Bradford, a husband battering in his wife's head with a hammer and then hanging himself, the parties, Thomas Bentley, a rope maker, about fifty years of age, and his wife, between 50 and 60 years of age, resided, along with their family – three young women and a young man – at 26, Boldshay Street, off Maperton Road, were to all appearances in fairly comfortable circumstances.

Such horrible tragedies as this are but too frequent in our crowded towns. They are of a dismal sameness. The perpetrators are not desperate criminals that prey on the public; but persons whose lives have turned sour and gloomy for want of healthy living, or through brooding suspicion until at last the storm breaks in the murder of the weaker partner of their lot, and the suicide of her assailant.

This is one of the darkest chapters in the subjection of women. This class of crime also reveals a weakness in our national life as at present constituted. Of true neighbourliness there is too little in big towns, and when estrangement sets in there are too often – so isolated are the lives of many people – no friends to step in and heal the breach, which goes on widening until it ends in a ghastly catastrophe. The world hears the story, learns that the parties are in humble life, that the details are sordid and common-place, and resumes its business. But it should be the concern of professional philanthropists and reformers to seek to prevent domestic quarrels from proceeding to such a height.

Bradford Daily Telegraph
Thursday 19 January 1894

The Murder

Thomas Bentley was, as far as some neighbours were generally concerned, a quiet and respectable man. He was a member of the Blue Ribbon Army (a society dedicated to temperance) and, by all accounts, a frequent churchgoer – a regular pillar of society, some might say. However, behind this thin veil of respectability he had a vicious, jealous temperament, which he regularly directed towards his fifty-seven-year-old, long suffering

Terrible Tragedy in Bradford, *The Illustrated Police News*, Saturday 27 January 1894.

wife. Recently, his foul temper had induced Sarah Bentley to leave him and stay with her neice, Mrs Thompson. She had, however, been forced to return to the marital home just six days before the dreadful murder because Thomas had made it clear that if she didn't, then he would surely 'murder her and everyone else belonging to them'.

Life hadn't always been so volatile in the Bentley household, and there had once been great love between the couple. They were married twenty-seven years previous, quite romantically on Christmas Day, and had taken their vows at Bradford Cathedral. Thomas, who was born in Salford, Lancashire, was nearly five years younger than Sarah, whose maiden name was Tunstall. Sarah, like her husband, originated from Lancashire, although she was born in Lancaster. The couple had produced three daughters and two sons, of which only the daughters and one son were still living. Their eldest son, James, had died in April 1884, aged fifteen, which could go far to explain why his father's personality had changed over the previous decade. But this was Victorian Bradford, and child mortality was, to some degree, both expected and accepted. The family had lived at No. 50 Heap Street for many years, before moving to Boldshay Street in 1891. The house at Boldshay Street was a typical Bradford back-to-back type cottage, two storeys high, containing two bedrooms and an attic, and was furnished very comfortably, considering the family's income and expenditure.

Despite the recent difficulties, the couple on the morning of 19 January 1894 appeared to have patched up their differences and, as far as their children were concerned, were 'on the best of terms'. As was the routine of the Bentley household, the elder children departed for work in the morning, leaving their parents alone at home together. Thomas, whose regular employment was that of a rope maker, was at that time unemployed, and had been so for some five months or more.

So, it was with some surprise that the couple's fifteen-year-old son, who was also called Thomas, returned home at twenty minutes past twelve for some dinner to find the house locked and the blinds closed. After getting no response from his knocks at the door, Thomas junior, who was employed as a roller shutter maker, wasted no time in sliding down the coal shoot and entered the house via the cellar head, which lead directly into the kitchen.

What he saw was to haunt the young lad for the rest of his life. He found his mother lying dead on the floor with terrible head injuries. Sarah was lying on her right side, with her head facing the front door and her feet close to the cellar head. About 3 feet away from his mother's body, he observed that a box that was normally on a shelf had been placed on the floor. The box contained various screws and nails. Taking in the enormity of the situation, the youngster stepped over his mother's body, exited the house via the front door, which was locked from the inside, and went to the local shop to raise the alarm.

The first Mrs Kench, the shopkeeper, knew of the awful tragedy was when Thomas junior thrust his head through the open shop doorway and cried 'I believe mi' mother's dead'. At once Mrs Kench hurried to the house with young Thomas, and no sooner had she crossed the threshold than she came across the lifeless body of her neighbour. She cried, 'Yes, Thomas, thy mother's dead; run and fetch a doctor and the police.' Horrified by the scene presented to her, Mrs Kench left the house in complete shock.

Within minutes of Mrs Kench leaving, young Thomas arrived back at the house at 12.40 p.m. in the company of PC Heaton. The constable observed that Sarah's head had horrific injuries, and she was lying in a pool of blood. PC Heaton then carried out a thorough search of the house with a view to locating Thomas Bentley senior, for it followed that given the door was locked from the inside, the husband must still be there. He found nothing on the first floor and so ventured up the stairs into the small attic, where he discovered the husband's body suspended by a rope attached to the ceiling. On the floor of the attic near the body, the constable found a short, heavy hammer, the type generally used at that time for breaking up coal. The hammer was covered in blood. Dr Gray, whose surgery was close by in Barkerend Road, confirmed life was extinct in both husband and wife, and that they had been dead for some time, their bodies being cold. The husband's body was then cut down and laid on the floor beside that of Sarah, awaiting the arrival of the ambulance, which then conveyed the bodies to the mortuary.

Dr Lodge, the police surgeon, found the wife's head to have serious injuries conducive to her death. The husband, a rope-maker, had made one abortive attempt to take his own life, but ironically found the cord too weak and, after taking it from his neck, he then used a piece of rope attached to a hook in the ceiling to achieve his own death.

Immediately after the discovery of the tragedy, the Bentleys' daughters were sent for. The two elder daughters were beside themselves with grief when they heard the news. The younger of the two, Sarah, who was employed at a mill in Springfield Street, was totally devastated, as was Mary Elizabeth, who was employed as a barmaid at St James's Hotel. She wept uncontrollably and had to be assisted to leave the hotel by one of the waitresses. Both the girls were conveyed in cabs to the house of a Mrs Kershaw, who was a close family friend.

As the motive for the crime was at best vague, a *Telegraph* reporter went to the house in the hope that the girls might be willing to make a statement. When the reporter entered, the eldest girl, Mary Elizabeth, was seated in an armchair with her head resting on the table. She was weeping hysterically. When she was informed of the presence of the reporter she made an effort to compose herself, and succeeded to a certain point. She could give no particularly clear reason for the crime committed by her father, but said he had a nasty temper. She was not at home on the night previous, and therefore could not say if there had been any bigger quarrel than usual, although she feared as much. She had never seen her father strike her mother in the whole of the time she resided at home, but on several occasions she had seen him raise his hand in anger, as though he intended to strike her. On these occasions, it was only through the interference of one of the children that her mother was not knocked about. The young woman then completely broke down and lost control of her emotions.

The reporter sought out the Bentley's neighbours, who revealed that Sarah Bentley was held in high esteem as a decent and amiable person. As regards the man, the neighbours knew very little about him other than he was quiet and gave them no trouble.

The reporter asked: 'Do you think there is any reason to think the woman was likely to make her husband jealous?' 'Oh, no, not at all. There could not be a nicer woman – no, I should never have thought her likely to cause her husband jealousy.'

'What about the husband? What sort of a man was he?' 'Well, I never had much to do with him. He was always very quiet, so far as I know.'

'Was he irritable?' 'Well, I think he must have been, or else he wouldn't have done this.'

'Have you ever heard them quarrelling?' 'No, I've never heard any disturbance whatever.'

Shortly after the bodies had been removed to the mortuary, the reporter saw Thomas Bentley junior at the house of a cousin, Mrs Thompson, in Trafalgar Street. Predictably, Thomas was overcome with grief after the loss of his parents and the terrible experience he had just gone through. He told the reporter that his father was extremely jealous and was continually threatening his mother. However, the night before, nothing unusual occurred to arouse any suspicions that he would carry out any of his threats, and the family went to bed early. Mrs Thompson was able to shed more light into the affairs of the family. She said: '[Her] aunt and Bentley had been married for about twenty-five years. The first few years of their married life was spent happily, but at least ten years ago the husband became extremely jealous of his wife, and since then she had been repeatedly subject to ill treatment, and more

No. 26 Boldshay Street.

than once she had left him and went to reside with friends, but he always persuaded her to return to him. The poor woman bore his treatment almost without a murmur, although he had no cause to suspect her of infidelity. Occasionally, however, she would complain to Mrs Thompson of his ill usage. A week ago yesterday he was in a violent temper, and threatened to do for his wife. During the night he became extremely outrageous, and the eldest daughter had to rise and restore peace. The following day, Mrs Bentley visited Mrs Thompson's house, where she remained until night. She was afraid to stop with her husband alone during the day, as she believed it was his intention to take her life. She returned home with one of her children, and since then peace seems to have reigned until this morning. Bentley was inclined to be idle, and it is stated that he would not work although he was offered it, preferring to live on the earnings of his sons and daughters. Mrs Bentley was much respected by her neighbours.'

The Investigation

On Monday 23 January, Mr J. G. Hutchinson, jun., the deputy borough coroner, opened the inquiry into the terrible affair that took place in Bradford on Friday 19 January 1894, which resulted in the murder of Sarah Bentley and the subsequent suicide of the murderer, her husband, Thomas Bentley, Boldshay Street, Barkerend Road.

The jury were sworn in at eleven o'clock, and then proceeded to view the bodies at the mortuary. On their return to the courtroom at noon, the examination of witnesses commenced. Chief Inspector Dobson watched the inquiry on behalf of the police.

Thomas Bentley junior, son of the two deceased, was called first. He said he was a revolving shutter maker. His mother was fifty-seven years of age. He last saw her alive on the night of Thursday last, at about half-past ten. Witness did not see her prior to his leaving for work on Friday morning. His father retired to rest before him on Thursday evening, and when he went to bed, he left his mother and youngest sister, Ann Ellen, in the kitchen. On Friday, he left for work at half-past six and returned home to dinner about twenty minutes past twelve. Thomas then told the inquest the circumstances surrounding his discovery of his mother's body. He then went on to give some background information to his parent's relationship and said the last time he knew of his mother and father having words was a week past Thursday last. His mother told him that she and his father had been quarrelling. His father was not present when she informed him of the quarrel. He had heard his mother and father quarrel frequently. His father appeared to be of a jealous disposition, and alleged that he heard men whistling after his wife. He had never heard his father threaten his mother. His father had been out of employment for about twenty weeks. Ever since a week last Friday, his father appeared to be strange in his manner. He was melancholy and seemed disinclined to talk. Before this, he had observed on many occasions that his father was strange in his ways. Last Thursday night, the family were sitting in the kitchen together. His father was present, but he was very quiet. He did not appear to be ill. At seven o'clock, he went upstairs and did not return that night. When he discovered his mother on the Friday afternoon, she was dead. There was nothing to indicate that a struggle had taken place in the kitchen. He said he knew the hammer (then produced), and that it belonged to his father and was used principally for breaking coals. He did not know where it was on the Friday morning when he left for work.

Twenty-eight-year-old Thomas Little, gardener, Boldshay Street, said he knew Mrs Bentley and her husband. They had lived as neighbours over the past three years. So far as he knew, they had not lived very happily together. Thomas said he did not see Mrs Bentley alive on Friday, but he saw the husband between nine and ten o'clock. He was in the backyard, and was smoking. He did not see him alive again. He heard no quarrel that morning, all being quiet.

Mrs Jackson, the attendant at the public mortuary, said that at three o'clock last Friday she laid out the body of the deceased, Mrs Bentley. It was well nourished. Her skull was completely smashed in on the top at the right side, and there was a large wound on her forehead. On the right side of the cheek there was a black bruise, and the back of the left hand was also bruised. Considerable force must have been used to cause the injuries to the head. On the top of the skull there was a mark of a hammer head, and she thought the hammer produced might easily have caused the wounds.

PC Heaton stated that from the information he received from Thomas Bentley junior, he proceeded to No. 26 Boldshay Street at 12.40 p.m. He found Mrs Bentley dead upon the floor. Her head was in a pool of blood, and he found the hammer in the attic. PC Heaton said he went upstairs and found the husband suspended by the rope now shown. The constable minutely explained how the rope was fastened round the dead man's neck. He assisted to cut down the body. Bentley's toes just touched the floor.

Chief Inspector Dobson said that on Friday last he was called to No. 26 Boldshay Street, about half-past one. There he found PC Heaton in possession of the house. Mrs Bentley was laid dead upon the floor. In his opinion, from the position of the woman and the appearance of the furniture, there had been no struggle between husband and wife. He believed the first blow from the hammer, which was blood-stained, had killed Mrs Bentley.

Dr Samuel Lodge said he went to Boldshay Street Friday last and saw the deceased woman. He raised the head, and saw a large circular wound in the forehead. There was another of considerably greater dimensions on the top of the head. Another wound had been inflicted on the back of the head, similar to the one on the forehead. He found afterwards that the skull was fractured. The right side of the woman's head lay in a large clot of blood, which defined the outline of the face exactly. The hammer produced would be a likely instrument to cause such wounds as he had described. The woman's tongue protruded, and was fixed tightly between her teeth, one of which was broken. Her face and extremities were cold, but the body was slightly warm.

The foreman said any of the three blows would have been sufficient to kill the woman. In his opinion, she was struck from behind.

This concluded the evidence so far as the deceased woman was concerned.

The coroner, in summing up, said the injuries could not have been accidentally inflicted. The jury returned a verdict of 'wilful murder' against the husband. The jury also returned a verdict on Thomas Bentley, that he, having murdered his wife, then committed suicide while temporarily insane.

On Tuesday 23 January 1894, the funerals of Thomas and Sarah Bentley took place at Scholemoor Cemetery. Quite bizarrely, Sarah was buried in the same grave as that of her husband. The relatives of the couple, with a view to keeping the funeral a family affair, took every precaution to keep the details a secret, but it was futile. It was arranged that the cortège would leave from the mortuary rather than the family home. Earlier that morning, the bodies had been placed in coffins made of polished pitch pine, and were laid side by side. The lid of the husband's coffin bore the following inscription:

THOMAS BENTLEY
Died January 19, 1894
Aged 53 years.

An inscription had also been engraved on the top of his wife's coffin. It read:

SARAH BENTLEY
Died January 19th, 1894
Aged 57.

The funeral party assembled at the house of Sarah Bentley's cousin in Trafalgar Street. There Mr J. W. Elders, the leader of the Gospel Union, conducted a small service. Five cabs conveyed the son, Thomas Bentley, the three daughters, and the other relatives to the mortuary, where they joined the hearses, which arrived at the same time. The coffin containing the body of the husband was placed in the leading hearse. Mrs Bentley's remains were carried in the second hearse. Lots of people who had seen the cabs leave Trafalgar Street followed, and were joined on the journey by hundreds more as word that the funeral was to take place spread rapidly. Memorial cards were sold by young lads stationed at different points along the route taken by the procession, which made its way to Scholemoor Cemetery by way of Thornton Road, Listerhills Road, and Legrams Road, arriving at the cemetery gates at half-past two. By this time, the large crowd that had assembled, which was chiefly composed of women, followed in the wake of the carriages, and entered the grounds of Scholemoor. The coffins were taken to the non-conformist mortuary chapel, where Mr Elders conducted another service, to which only relatives were admitted.

The coffins were placed in one grave that was 9 feet deep. Mrs Bentley's coffin was covered with floral wreaths. Messrs Kirby and Acres, of Heaton Road, carried out the funeral arrangements. Order was maintained among the crowd by five policemen and the cemetery workmen.

The unmarked grave of Bentley at Scholemoor Cemetery, positioned between the two gravestones in the foreground.

Lister Bastow
Double Murder and Suicide, 1897

WIFE AND DAUGHTER KILLED AT DUDLEY HILL
THE MURDERER CUTS HIS OWN THROAT

Yesterday afternoon a shocking murder suicide took place in Butler Street at Dudley Hill. The culprit was named Lister Bastow, and resided with his wife and daughter, the latter a girl 16 years of age. It appears that the murderer, who was an elderly man, killed his wife and daughter by cutting both their throats in a horrible fashion, the head of the girl being nearly severed, presenting a horrible sight. There were two young children in the house at the time, and after he had committed the dreadful act he took his own life in the same way.

Bradford Daily Telegraph
Friday 8 February 1897

The Murder

Lister Bastow wasn't just a jealous man, he was also a lazy oaf – well, that was just one opinion. His own mother thought him to be a harmless lad, but he was driven insane by money worries. One neighbour reported that as much as his wife begged him to get a job, only the imminent prospect of starvation would induce him to do something about it. A friend commented that he was prepared to sit in bed all day reading instead of earning a living, and if he ever got any complaints from his wife, he thought nothing at all of knocking her about.

It is certainly true that only a few weeks prior to this horrific murder, the forty-two-year-old spent his days sat in the barbers boasting of how his daughter was a capital worker providing for the family, although that may have just been bravado. There were many conflicting accounts relating to family life in the Bastow household; some thought him a monster, others didn't. What could possibly be true is that Bastow was suffering from depression, which was aggravated by the family's extreme poverty. Unfortunately, things came to a head when the bailiffs entered the family home on a warrant of £5 for rent arrears just days before the murders were committed. Not only did the bailiffs remove the majority of the family's furniture, they also took Mrs Bastow's mangle and other equipment she needed to perform her job taking in washing.

After this most recent humiliation, his wife Pricilla made up her mind to take the children and move in with her mother at Drighlinghton. When she informed her husband of her decision, it would prove to be a fatal mistake, one that would cost her

The scene of the crime: Butler Street, Dudley Hill. The cross on the gate marks the house of the murder.

her life and the life of her child. The first indication that anything was amiss in the Bastow household was when a shrill scream was heard emanating from the house in the early hours of 7 February. The next-door neighbour, a Mrs Briley, even identified the scream as coming from the couple's eldest daughter, Alice, yet she did nothing about it. Some justification for the lack of action by the neighbour was the fact that, during the previous eleven months that the Bastows had resided at Butler Street, the couple had frequently been heard to be arguing. In any event, even intervention at this stage would have been futile, for the foul deed was already done. Eventually, at around dinnertime the same day, Mrs Briley noticed that the blinds were drawn fully down, and there was a complete lack of movement from the usually busy household. Feeling a little uneasy, she decided to inform the landlord, Mr Charles Ratcliffe, who lived at the bottom of the street. Mr Ratcliffe was immediately concerned about the welfare of the tenants of his house, and with his suspicions strongly aroused he went to see Pricilla Bastow's mother before contacting Sergeant Simpson, who was stationed at Tong Street, Dudley Hill. As soon as Sergeant Simpson had taken the report, he acted on impulse and hurriedly went with the landlord to inspect the house.

Lister Bastow's attack on his family. *Inset*: The discovery of his body.

The first glimpse the sergeant caught of the house was enough to realise that all was not well. Walking to the doorway and raising the fanlight, he looked inside, though as the window of the interior of the house was in semi-darkness he struggled to get a good view. Taking his time and letting his eyes grow accustomed to the darkness, he carefully surveyed the limited area open to his vision until he saw what appeared to be a semi-naked body lying partially hidden by the door.

It was clear to him that the body was lifeless, and as a result he left to obtain further police assistance. Along with the landlord, the sergeant went in search of a constable, and was lucky to almost immediately come across PC Chesterton. The three men then made their way back to the house to force an entry. This was easily accomplished by breaking a cellar window, which allowed the three men to go straight inside the house, making their way firstly to the doorway where they found Pricilla Bastow in her nightdress. Her throat had been brutally cut and she was lying in a large pool of blood in an awkward position, with her right arm under her head. Her throat had been cut almost from ear to ear, but more deeply on the right side; she had virtually been decapitated. It was quite clear to the police that she had been brutally murdered.

While on the stairs, the men also discovered the body of Alice Bastow, and in front of the living room lay the body of Lister Bastow. All three family members had similar wounds in that their throats had been cut from ear to ear. Alice Bastow was laid upon her right side, with her jugular vein completely severed. She was in her night attire, and it was evident that she had just risen from her bed. After this very gruesome discovery, the three men again retraced their steps and went to the front living room.

There, the body of Lister was found lying on his front, dressed only in his shirt and socks. He was positioned near a table in the centre of the room with his head in the middle of a large pool of blood; a razor was found open on either side of him. Of all the bodies discovered, his was the only one that appeared to still have signs of life.

The officers immediately summoned medical aid and, within a few minutes, Doctor Brand had arrived. He found the body of the man to be fairly warm but quite dead. The other two bodies were stone cold. From this and the postures of the bodies, there could be no doubt that Bastow had quarrelled with his wife early in the morning and, while in the doorway, deliberately cut her throat. She likely resisted, for it must have been the sounds of a scuffle that drew the attention of the daughter Alice, who had apparently just left her bed to come to her mother's aid. She had been sleeping in the upstairs bedroom along with two younger children, Janie, aged eight, and Tom, aged five, who, on the arrival of the constables, were found to have been spared and were sleeping quietly in a small bedroom, unaware of the tragedy.

The Investigation

News of the fatalities had quickly spread through the town, prompting the arrival of reporters from the *Bradford Daily Telegraph* and other newspapers at the scene. The shocked neighbours wasted no time in condemning Lister Bastow as the murderer.

'Had Bastow been a jealous man?' asked one reporter.

'Oh! He was shocking!' said one neighbour, 'his wife Pricilla told me herself. She said he had been jealous ever since the first day they were married.'

'Had he any cause for jealousy, do you think?'

'Oh dear, no!' replied the neighbour, 'there could never be a nicer or more upright woman.'

Mr Ratcliffe, the landlord, explained to the reporter that when the Bastows' immediate neighbour brought him the news that the blinds were still down and there had been no signs of anyone stirring, he decided to set off in his pony cart to Atherton, where Mrs Bastow's mother lived. The old lady knew something bad had happened as soon as she saw him and she started weeping. Through the tears, she said, 'Whatever is the matter, mister?'

Mr Ratcliffe replied, 'I don't know, I've come to find out.' Later a *Telegraph* reporter managed to get into conversation with a friend of Lister Bastow at Dudley Hill police station. The friend had for some time visited the Bastows' house every Saturday night, and had seen nothing wrong with the man – as far as he knew, the couple had been very happy. To his three children he was as kind as a father could possibly be, and despite having appeared to be slightly depressed over the past few weeks, he had not turned to drink.

Mr and Mrs Nicholls, who lived in the house directly behind the Bastow residence, described Lister as being very quick tempered, but having only occasionally quarrelled with his wife. Of late, however, he had treated her well, and the couple went on to say, 'Lister Bastow preferred to go about dressed up rather than work. He would, in fact, have liked to have been a gentleman, but lacked the means. The murdered woman Priscilla was considered to be a good looking woman, but did not mix much with the neighbours.'

Mr Nicholls then went on to give some background information and stated,

Bastow was born in Bradford, and his mother lives in Fitzgerald Street, Bradford. His brother keeps a grocer's shop in the town. Bastow's wife came from Drighlington, where her mother, Mrs Whitehead, still resides. For a time, he and his wife lived apart. About last Easter, they were reconciled, and Bastow took the house in Butler Street, where they have since lived together. The children lived during the separation of their parents with their grandmother at Drighlington, but the whole family was reunited upon the reconciliation of husband and wife. Bastow had been employed by Messrs Walter Brearley and Sons, stuff manufacturers, Prospect Mills, Tong Street. Some time ago, however, he lost his work, but he afterwards succeeded in obtaining employment from a firm of electrical engineers in Bradford. Whilst

LISTER BASTOW.

An illustration taken from a photograph, which is a perfect likeness of Lister Bastow at the time of the murder.

following this employment he is said (but this is not altogether believed) to have broken a lot of glasses, and to have had to work for nine weeks without wages in order to make up the damage. At the end of that time – not quite three weeks ago – he was dismissed, and he has since been out of work. His wife has taken in a little washing, and the eldest daughter worked as a weaver at Messrs Brearley and Sons' mills until the day preceding the murder. The two younger children attended Tong Street National School, and on Sunday the Holme Lane Congregational Sunday school and chapel.

Further information as to the family's circumstances came from Mrs Bastow, the mother of Lister Bastow. Described as a homely and good-looking woman, Mrs Bastow was beside herself with grief at the awful crime committed by her son. She told the reporter that he had been born on 1 February 1852, making him forty-two years of age, and had married Pricilla Whitehead, daughter of Thomas Whitehead, at Kirkgate chapel seventeen years previously. At the time of the marriage, they were a happy couple. On being asked about his drinking habits, she made it clear that he had never during his whole life been tempted by strong drink. Of an exceedingly quiet disposition and not easily angered, he was fond of his wife and children. Mrs Bastow did point out that he was inclined to laziness, and that in her opinion it was his only known fault. He had had a good upbringing, but never seemed willing

Kirkdale Wesleyan chapel.

to work much. The reporter then went on to enquire as to how she could account for the terrible crimes he had committed. In tears she responded, 'It's all through poverty and the threat his wife had made to leave him and go back to her mother's house. They must have quarrelled during the night about it, and before allowing her to leave him he had taken her life. He must have been insane, for he was always a harmless lad.'

As the police investigation intensified, the excitement created in the Dudley Hill district by the horrific murders and suicide continued to draw in spectators from far and wide. The crime was the sole topic of conversation in Butler Street and the surrounding neighbourhood for days. Groups of people stood staring at the exterior of the crime scene, which no one was allowed to enter apart from relatives and the police. The bodies of the victims and that of Bastow were laid out side by side together in a downstairs room in readiness for the funerals, which were planned to take place the day after the inquest. All the blood that splattered the staircase walls had been removed and the house cleaned. Pricilla's brother arrived from Drighlington and made all the funeral arrangements for his sister and niece.

According to medical opinion at the time, Alice more than likely died first and the mother afterwards. At the time of the discovery of their bodies, it appeared that both had been dead for between ten and twelve hours. Rigor mortis had set in in both cases, and was more profound in Alice. Bastow's body was still warm, and had been dead for no more than two hours before he was discovered. On inspecting his bed, the police found it still warm, which inclined investigators to believe that, bizarrely, having committed the murders he simply went back to bed, for a few hours at least. It was certain that he had washed his hands at the sink at the cellar head, as blood evidence was found both in the basin and upon the towel he used to dry himself. It later transpired that a coal hawker had called during the morning and it was supposed that Lister had committed suicide soon after this event at midday. Besides slashing his wife's throat, he had stabbed her repeatedly in the breast. The marital bed in which the couple slept was saturated with blood, which proved that Mrs Bastow was first attacked in bed, but managed to escape downstairs, and was caught by Lister before she could escape the house. Evidence relating to the murder of his daughter led the investigation team to believe she had been easily overpowered by her father.

On Friday 8 February at Holme Lane Hotel, Dudley Hill, Mr Thomas Taylor, coroner in the Wakefield district, presided over the inquest into the circumstances surrounding the deaths of Lister Bastow, his wife Priscilla, and his daughter Alice. The jury, having been sworn in, viewed the bodies of the deceased. Mr Abraham Elsworth acted as foreman. Superintendent Crawshaw watched the inquiry on behalf of the West Riding police authorities. Percy Ross Whitehead, joiner, Whitehall Road, Drighlington, was the first witness called. He said,

Pricilla Bastow was my sister, Alice Bastow was my niece, and Lister Bastow was my brother-in-law. Lister Bastow was by occupation a weaving overlooker. My sister was thirty-nine years of age in June last. Alice was sixteen last October, and wrought as a worsted weaver. I have not seen Lister Bastow for twelve months. I saw his body yesterday. Ever since they left Eccleshill about three years ago, they have been repeatedly at variance. So far as I know, he did a 'bit' of drinking, but I have not seen him the worse for liquor. My sister lived with my mother about six months. She was accompanied by Alice and the other two children. I last saw my sister alive in March, when she returned to Lister. Priscilla was in Drighlington a few weeks ago, but I did not see her. Word of the murder reached my mother yesterday afternoon, but I did not know until after six o'clock. When I was informed of what had occurred, I proceeded to Butler Street. I saw the three bodies, which I had no difficulty in identifying. I never heard that Lister Bastow's mind was deranged. My sister never complained about her husband.

Mary Butler, wife of Seth Butler, butcher, of No. 297 Tong Street, was next examined. She said:

I have known Mrs Bastow since she came to my husband's shop and washed for me at home. On Monday evening last, Jane, the little girl, brought back the clothes unwashed, and said her mother was unable to wash them because the landlord had taken away the things. I know Mrs Bastow had threatened to leave her husband, and I asked them to come and see me on the Tuesday night. They came, and both appeared to have been crying; in fact, I never saw people in such distress as they were. Mrs Bastow seemed to be sadly 'put out' about her home. I asked what she intended doing, because she had told me that if her husband broke up another home she would never live with him again. She was at first almost unable to speak, but latterly said she was going to Drighlington with her family. She cried bitterly, and I said, 'You seem upset about leaving him.' She replied 'Yes, I am, he has not a friend in the world.' I asked her what Bastow intended doing. She answered that he could stop in the house for a fortnight, when their notice was up, but after that she did not know what he would do. I believe they had lived a very disagreeable life for months past. After she left my house, I never saw her alive again.

John Thomas Brearley, stuff manufacturer, Butler Street, said he had been acquainted with the Bastows for about twelve months. He saw Alice leave his mill about four o'clock on Tuesday afternoon. She appeared bright and cheerful, but it was evident she was in trouble. Lister Bastow was a weaving overlooker in his place for about six months. His father had dismissed him. The weavers formed a deputation and came to his father and saying they would not work under him because he (Bastow) was impudent and indolent. Ever since they came to live in Butler Street, Bastow had quarrelled with his wife. The rows between them generally occurred around midnight. The witness had heard Mrs Bastow cry to her husband 'take your hands off', and they could hear them running about the room as if he was chasing her. He had also heard Lister say, 'Come to bed, will you?' to which Mrs Bastow replied 'I won't go to bed with such a man as you.' The last quarrel he heard was on the night of Saturday last, between eleven and twelve o'clock. Alice had gone dozens of times to her work as if she had cried much during the night. Bastow appeared to have a nasty temper.

Dr William Thomas Brand was called next. He said he had examined the bodies of the three deceased. On the pillow under which the woman's stockings were found, there was a quantity of blood. He found the man's throat cut, and the fingers on the left hand injured. The wound to the throat was deep, and 5½ inches in length. The windpipe had been severed, and there was another cut on the windpipe an inch and a half below the deep gash. Eight little tentative cuts were visible at the left angle of the fatal wound, as if Bastow had been reluctant to go deeper. The right jugular vein was cut partly through, but not one of the large arteries was divided. The man was muscular and appeared to have been in the best of health. The wounds were undoubtedly self-inflicted. The body was very warm, and he had died within two hours of the discovery. Mrs Bastow was scarcely cold on the left breast. The cut to her throat extended almost all the way round the neck. The windpipe was cut completely through, and it had appeared as if the razor had been slashed in all directions. She could not possibly have inflicted the wounds with her own hand. On the back of the right hand was a cut that penetrated to the bone. The body was emaciated. There were two oblique wounds on Alice's throat – the upper cut was 3½ inches in length and penetrated through the skin to the top of the windpipe. An inch to the left of the top wound was the second cut, extending down for 5½ inches and almost reaching to the top of the right lung. Death must have ensued within two minutes of the wounds having been inflicted. Either of the razors would have been sufficient to cause the wounds sustained by both of the deceased. Cuts were visible on both the girls' hands, as if they had been put up to save her throat.

The coroner having summed up, the jury returned a verdict of 'wilful murder' against Bastow, and found a verdict of *felo de se* in his case.

On 10 February, the funerals of Lister Bastow, his wife and daughter took place. Lister was buried at Scholemoor Cemetery, and the mother and daughter at Drighlington. Lister's body had been collected from Butler Street late the night before and taken to his mother's house. At 10 a.m. prompt, the hearse, followed by two cabs containing the deceased's relatives, left his mother's house. With the exception of a small crowd that gathered when the hearse stopped at the door, the funeral attracted no attention.

A general view of Scholemoor Cemetery, where Lister Bastow was interred.

The Bradford Midland Hotel
Murder or Suicide, 1897

STRANGE AFFAIR IN BRADFORD
TWO PERSONS FOUND DEAD AT THE MIDLAND HOTEL

A grim discovery was made which created some consternation among the members of staff and the residents at a late hour last Friday night at the Midland Hotel, Bradford. At about a quarter to twelve a page boy named Alfred Ruddock went to the lavatory in the basement of the building and was horrified at finding a human foot projecting from the bottom of the service lift, which is close by.

He rushed at once in a terrible state of alarm and informed several members of the staff at the shocking discovery he had made. On becoming acquainted with the nature of the grim find, the sub manager caused investigations to be made, with the result that the bruised and disfigured remains of two members of the staff were found lying in the bottom of the lift.

Bradford Illustrated Weekly Telegraph
Saturday 18 August 1894

The Incident

Was young Rose murdered by her male co-worker? Did she perhaps spurn his romantic advances, and did this result in her untimely death followed by his suicide? Was it a freak accident? Did they both somehow fall in? What really happened?

As this is the last account to be entered into this book, I have decided to leave the reader with a highly speculative mystery to investigate. Although the event occurred nearly 120 years ago, the crime scene still exists, as do the contemporary newspaper accounts, recording the minute details of the fatalities. When the deaths were originally investigated, no one really knew for sure what had happened at the Midland Hotel on the night of Friday 10 August 1894, when two junior members of staff were found dead at the bottom of the service lift (dumb waiter) shaft in the hotel basement. So let us take a step back in time and re-examine the evidence presented at the time of the inquest in an attempt to solve what the great Victorian detectives and the coroner's inquiry could not. The victims of this tragic event were two teenagers, seventeen-year-old Rose Penistan and George F. Schelter, who was also of the same age. George, who originated from Nuremburg, Bavaria, had only been in Bradford for a fortnight prior to the event and was employed at the hotel as a junior waiter. Rose

The Midland Hotel under construction in 1889.

had held her position as the second still-room maid (a female servant who worked in the functional room in large houses and hotels where drinks and jams were made) for a period of about three months. When the disfigured victims of this freakish tragedy were discovered by Alfred Ruddock at a quarter to midnight, the pair had not been seen for nearly two hours and had only been noted as missing for about one hour. It was at first supposed that Schelter and Penistan had been sitting together on the edge of the service lift barrier by which the well of the lift was guarded, and by some means they lost their balance and had fallen into the basement. That was the most plausible view taken at the time, and this was despite the fact the opening was only 2 feet 3 inches wide and they would have probably found themselves wedged together in the shaft. Some weight was given to this theory because for anyone wanting to sit down in the room, this would have been the most convenient place to do so, and if they were to overbalance they would fall to the basement, a staggering 29 feet below. Both victims were found to have multiple injuries, including fractures to the skull, and one of Schelter's arms was broken. Following the removal of the bodies to the mortuary by the police, Rose Penistan was identified by her mother and siblings. A devastated and heartbroken Mrs Penistan, who was susceptible to fits anyway, had to be forcibly held down for about 5 minutes by four people at the sight of her daughter.

The coroner's enquiry is transcribed verbatim below.

The Investigation

THE INQUEST

At the Bradford Town Hall on Monday August 14, 1894 the Borough Coroner (Mr James Gwynne Hutchinson) held an inquest on Rose Penistan (17) still room maid, and George F Shelter (17) , waiter, both employed and residing till Friday night last, at the Midland Hotel, where they were killed by the dinner hoist. The jury were sworn, and then proceeded to view the scene of the fatality.

The jury, after their visit to the Midland Hotel, drove to the various places where the bodies were awaiting their view. They were away more than an hour, and it was nearly half past four before they returned and commenced the inquest.

Mr Young (Messrs Beale & Co., Birmingham) watched the case for the Midland Railway Company, and Mr John Waugh, Civil Engineer (retained by the Coroner) was also in attendance.

Mr Young at the outset expressed on behalf of the Midland Company and Mr Towle, their hotel manager, their regret at the occurrence, and their sympathy with the relatives of the deceased.

John Penistan, 11 Newton Street, Lincoln, said he was a plumber and the deceased woman was his sister. She was 17 years old, and was a domestic servant. She had, he thought, been at the Midland Hotel since May last. He had seen her dead body today in the public mortuary.

The dumb waiter in the Midland Hotel.

THE DISCOVERY OF THE BODIES

Alfred Ruddock, hoist attendant at the Midland Hotel, said he had charge of the passenger lift. He found the bodies of the deceased persons on Friday night about 11.45. They were in the basement pantry at the bottom of the house. The hoist in question was the dinner lift.

The Coroner – Just tell me what you discovered? – I had gone into the pantry with an empty plate, which I'd had my supper on and I was turning round to come out when I was startled by seeing a foot, under the hoist, and I could not stir for a moment, sir, with the fright, and I could not scream.

The Coroner – what did you do then? – I gave information to Clarke, the cellar man.

The Coroner – What did he do? – He went to look, and said to me 'it's right, go tell someone,' and I went and told one of the porters.

Continuing, witness said that by the manager's directions information and was given to the police, who removed the bodies in the ambulance.

The Coroner – How long before had you seen the young woman? – In the morning, sir.

The Coroner – Not since the morning? – No, sir.

The Coroner – Have you any information, or do you know how the bodies got into the position in which they were found? – No, sir.

The restaurant at the Midland Hotel, pictured in 1890.

Henry Clarke, cellar man at the Midland Hotel, said on Friday night, in consequence of what Ruddock said to him, he went into the basement pantry. He saw a man's foot protruding from the bottom of the door at the side of the dinner lift. As soon as he saw the feet, he sent the cage of the lift up and then leant over to feel for the young man and was horrified to find that there was also a young woman there.

The only light was that from the electric light in the station. There were two pails at the bottom of the lift, and the young man was laid on one, and the girl was partly on her side and partly on the other pail. The girl's feet were in an opposite direction to those of the young man.

The cage of the lift was close upon the bodies. Witness shouted out to Ruddock to fetch help. The manager came, and with assistance he got the bodies out.

The Coroner – Had you seen Rose that day? – Yes I saw her about six o'clock in the still room.

The Coroner – So far as you know had the man any duties requiring him to be in the pantry, or still room? – His duties were in the coffee room, sir.

In reply to Mr Young, witness said he slept in a room next to the pantry on the side of the lift. He was in bed when Ruddock alarmed him. He went to bed about eleven o'clock, but had not been asleep and had heard no noise.

The Coroner – In your bedroom could you hear if the hoist was worked? – Yes sir.

The Coroner – Did you hear it worked after you went to bed? – No, sir.

The Coroner – Did you hear any noise in the hoist well? – No, sir.

The Foreman– I should like to ask if they were missed any length of time?

The Midland Hotel earlier this year, during filming of Michael Portillo's *Great British Railway Journeys*.

Witness said he had not seen the girl after six o'clock, and he had not seen the man for two or three days, and did not know he was missing.

Mr William O Audinwood, resident manager of the Midland Hotel, said the deceased was second still room maid. She had been at the hotel since the middle of May.

The Coroner – In connection with her duties, would she have to work the service hoist? – It would be impossible to work it from the still room, sir.

The Coroner – It would be no part of her duties? – No, sir.

The Coroner – Where was she principally employed? – All her duties were confined to the still room.

The Coroner – Now, referring to Friday. When did you last see her before her body was found? – I was in the still room a few minutes before ten o'clock.

The Coroner – Were any of the other maids there? – No, sir.

The Coroner – She was alone? – Yes, sir.

The Coroner – Now, was George Schelter a waiter? – Junior coffee room waiter, sir.

The Coroner – How long had he been at the hotel? – About a fortnight, sir.

The Coroner – Would his duties cause him to go into the still room? – Yes, sir.

The Coroner – Were you aware of him being at all acquainted with the deceased other than as a fellow servant? – No, sir.

The Coroner – Had the deceased girl a box at the hotel, or any place for private papers? – A box in her bedroom.

The Coroner – Has it been searched? – That has been given to her mother.

The Coroner – What time was it when you got into the pantry? – About a quarter to twelve, sir.

The Coroner – Who called you? – Well the rushing of two porters past the hall drew my attention. I was sitting in my office.

The Coroner – What did you find when you got there? – At the bottom of the lift I saw two bodies.

The Coroner – Now give me the position of the woman first? – I couldn't give the exact position, sir; I ran upstairs to telephone to the Town Hall.

Continuing, witness said that the feet of the man were right underneath the hoist lever, and the feet of girl were in the opposite direction.

In reply to further questions, witness said the clothes of both the deceased persons appeared to be in order.

On Friday night it was the head still room maid's evening off, and the deceased girl would be on duty from six to twelve, so that in the ordinary course of things she would be alone in the still room.

The Coroner – When you were in the still room there was no one else there? – No, there was a waiter just going into the coffee room from the still room.

The Coroner – So that if the waiter was in the still room, he would be properly about his duties? – Yes.

By Mr Young – What would be the effect of a person striking the hoist lever in falling down the shaft? – It would be to bring the cage down.

Since this accident have you with the use of the ladder gone up the shaft of the lift? – Yes.

Taking with you a light? – Yes.

And did you find a slipper anywhere? – Yes.

The Coroner – Where did you find the slipper? – On a small platform, level with the ground floor, half way between the still room floor and the basement.

Mr Young – Is that the place where the men stand to oil the machinery of the lift? – Yes.

Does it correspond with the other slipper found on the foot of the girl? – Yes.

Did you find any marks on the walls? – Down the front of the lift there were many scratches on the woodwork.

And did those appear to be recent? – Yes, sir.

Florence Ryalls, head still room maid at the Midland Hotel, said that the deceased girl worked under her. She last saw her alive at six o'clock on Friday evening, when she left her alone in the still room. Witness returned at five minutes to eleven and went to the still room, but there was no-one there. Witness asked the waiter on duty where she was, and he replied that he had not seen her since ten o'clock.

Joseph Engieler, a waiter at the Midland Hotel, said his duties were in the coffee room, and he knew the deceased. On Friday night he was on duty from eight o'clock until twelve. He last saw Schelter alive about ten o'clock, when he was just coming from the coffee room into the still room. He was going there with some butter dishes. The deceased girl was there, and witness left them there together, because he had to go into the coffee room. She was at the table, and he was on the other side putting the butter dishes away.

The Coroner – Did you as a fact see either of them afterwards alive? – No, sir.

The Coroner – How soon after that did you go into the still room? – About twenty minutes after.

The Coroner – Was either of them there? – There was no one there.

The Coroner – Did you inquire for the maid? – Not just then; I was able to manage by myself, but I made inquiries for Schelter a little later, but could learn nothing of him.

The Coroner – Have you at any time noticed any familiarity between them? – No, sir.

Mr John Waugh, Civil Engineer, said he had examined the hoist, which was a hydraulic one and double as far as the still room. The distance that the two deceased persons were supposed to have fallen was 29 feet. It was difficult to understand how two persons could sit on the barrier in the hoist opening, which was only 2 feet 3 inches wide. It was also difficult to understand how two persons could fall down the shaft together.

The circumstances must have been extraordinary, such as might be represented by two persons skylarking on the edge of a precipice. He had worked the hoist that morning, and it appeared to be in good working order. It was one of the very best constructed. Its working conditions were those which were usual in this class of hoist.

Mr Waugh added, 'The question arises, could not the opening be closed automatically by the cage, or vice versa? This arrangement has been very successfully applied in the case of hoists used by passengers or employees in our factories and workshops. It has also been tried for service lifts, and with this result, that the opening is being closed as the cage ascends or descends and that those who are taking out or putting something into the cage are very liable to be caught in a sort of double guillotine; and accidents have occurred in this way.

'If some hoist engineer or other inventor can so arrange the opening and closing of openings in connection with this class of hoist and avoid the liability to accidents to which I have referred, those who use the hoists would, I think, readily adopt them.'

Mr Young – On behalf of the company I can only say that if some engineer could contrive something which would make accidents impossible we should be very glad to adopt it.

Mr Samuel Lodge, police surgeon, said he had made a post mortem examination, in company with Dr James, Dr White and Dr Muatt, of the bodies. He found that the deceased girl Penistan had received a fracture of the skull and the breastbone. Death must have been instantaneous.

Inspector Ackroyd and Thomas Morrison, a waiter also gave evidence.

The Coroner then intimated that he would adjourn the further hearing of the case for a week.

Formal evidence of the identity of the deceased George F. Schelter was then taken. A distant relative named George Hermann, of 44 Hampstead Street, stated

James Gwynne Hutchinson, the Coroner for Bradford.

Mr J. G. Hutchinson.
The Coroner for Bradford.

that the deceased came from Nuremberg, Bavaria and had been in England about five months. The inquest was then adjourned until Monday next.

THE SECOND HEARING

The enquiry into the deaths of George F. Schelter (17) under-waiter, and Rose Peniston (17), second still-room maid at the Midland Hotel, Bradford, who were killed on the evening of Friday week by a dinner hoist at that hotel, was resumed by the borough coroner (Mr J. G. Hutchinson) at the Bradford Town Hall, on Monday.

At the previous hearing, the case of Rose Peniston was dealt with. On Monday, evidence in connection with the death of Schelter was called.

Henry Clark, the cellar man, repeated his evidence given on the previous hearing. He said that when he went into the basement pantry he found Schelter lying face downwards in the bottom of the hoist. His arm was held up, whilst the other was doubled under the body. The girl was lying on her back, and was partly on the top of Schelter's body. The girl's feet were in an opposite direction to those of Schelter's. When he got the bodies out, they were quite warm.

Dr Samuel Lodge said Schelter's face was blackened about the eyes and temples, and the right arm was fractured. There were a few scratches on the face, but the other injuries were so terrible that these were insignificant in character. The skull was broken to pieces. The brain was lacerated, and a circular piece of bone had been driven into the brain. Without a minute anatomical examination of all the bones of the head, it would be difficult to tell whether any one portion was whole.
The Coroner – A complete smash up? – Yes, sir.
Dr Lodge – The cause of death was fracture of the skull and laceration of the brain.

After a short absence, the jury returned an open verdict in both cases.

The remains of George F. Schelter were interred on 15 August 1894 at Scholemoor Cemetery. The funeral costs were paid for by the Midland Railway Company. The funeral of Rose Penistan took place in her home town in Lincolnshire.

The Midland Hotel, which is now owned by Peel Hotels, was built in the late 1880s as the jewel in the crown of the Midland Railway's northern operations. The iconic Victorian hotel is no stranger to drama, for in October 1905, the great Victorian actor Sir Henry Irving collapsed and died after an attack of syncope on the grand staircase, where he was attended to by Bram Stoker, the author of *Dracula*. The famous actor had just returned from the nearby Theatre Royal, where he appeared as 'Becket'. His last words on stage were: 'Into Thy Hands, O Lord, into Thy hands'

Fitting words indeed to end this book...